CHRISTIANS, FEMINISTS, AND THE CULTURE OF PORNOGRAPHY

ARTHUR J. MIELKE

UNIVERSITY
PRESS OF
AMERICA

Lanham • New York • London

Copyright © 1995 by
University Press of America,® Inc.
4720 Boston Way
Lanham, Maryland 20706

3 Henrietta Street
London WC2E 8LU England

All rights reserved
Printed in the United States of America
British Cataloging in Publication Information Available

Library of Congress Cataloging-in-Publication Data
Mielke, Arthur J.
Christians, feminists, and the culture of pornography /
by Arthur J. Mielke.
p.   cm.
Includes bibliographical references and index.
1. Pornography—Social aspects.   2. Pornography—Religious
aspects—Christianity.   3. Feminism.   I. Title.
HQ471.M63   1994   363.4'7—dc20   94–37690 CIP

ISBN 0–8191–9764–5 (cloth : alk. paper)
ISBN 0–8191–9765–3 (pbk. : alk. paper)

HQ
471
. M 63

1995

JESUIT - KRAUSS - McCORMICK - LIBRARY
1100 EAST 55th STREET
CHICAGO, ILLINOIS 60615

 ∞™ The paper used in this publication meets the minimum requirements of
American National Standard for Information Sciences—Permanence
of Paper for Printed Library Materials, ANSI Z39.48–1984.

To the Memory of Robert J. Stoller, M.D.

December 15, 1924—September 6, 1991

One rational voice is dumb: over a grave
The household of Impulse mourns one dearly loved.
Sad is Eros, builder of cities,
And weeping anarchic Aphrodite.

—W. H. Auden

Permissions:

Excerpt from "In Memory of Sigmund Freud," from *Collected Poems* by W. H. Auden, copyright © 1940 and renewed 1968 by W. H. Auden. Reprinted by permission of Random House, Inc.

Excerpt from *Vox*, by Nicholson Baker, copyright © 1992 by Random House, Inc.

Excerpt from "The Sentential Man" in *The Collected Poems of Theodore Roethke*, copyright © 1937, 1954, 1957, 1958, 1959, 1960, 1961, 1962, 1963, 1964, 1965, 1966 by Beatrice Roethke as Administratrix of the Estate of Theodore Roethke, by Doubleday, a division of Bantam Doubleday Dell Publishing Group, Inc.

Excerpt from "Coming Apart" in *You Can't Keep a Good Woman Down*, copyright © 1980 by Alice Walker, reprinted by permission of Harcourt Brace & Company.

Revised Standard Version of the Bible, copyright © 1946 by Division of Christian Education of the National Council of the Churches of Christ in the United States of America.

Contents

Preface

Several years ago while browsing in one of America's finest bookstores, Powell's Books of Portland, Oregon, I drifted innocently into the Feminism section and took *Take Back the Night: Women on Pornography* down from the shelf. Not realizing that this was a collection of writings exclusively by women opposed to pornography, I paged vainly through the text in search of at least one favorable estimation: was it possible that no women anywhere were willing to say a positive word about pornography or confess an interest in it? Stubborn male presumption and anecdotal reports from women friends caused me to doubt that I had encountered the full range of feminist perspectives on pornography and I began to search feminist literature for the other side of the story.

The combined influences of church life in the Reformed tradition and parental discomfort with sex compounded the furtiveness of my own early interest in sex: the spontaneous (and embarrassing) erections, the prurient desire to see the shadow of a woman's pubic hair in the negligee section of the Sears Roebuck catalogue, the masturbatory interludes that disrupted attempts to complete geometry homework—in short, an adolescence memorialized with humorous relief by Philip Roth in *Portnoy's Complaint*. Was there any female analogue for this kind of experience, I have since wondered, or were my brothers and I out there all alone, exposed and needy?

In my late 30s, after surrendering a career as a truck driver, I began a doctoral program in religion whose focus was the exploration of two areas of visceral reality I believed were troubling to mainline Protestant Christians like myself: sex and anger. Despite our best intentions, what many of us had been taught from those early days in Sunday school was being disrupted with great regularity by the recalcitrant interests of the body, even if with advancing age that body became more imaginal and less immediately physical. Could we as Christians be both religious and angry, both religious and sexual? Although I had not found formal church membership a satisfying commitment to maintain, I was never able to completely shake those theological questions. To my great benefit, my graduate school mentor did not flinch when I expressed an interest in writing about pornography, and I was able to pursue to its formal conclusion the dissertation research that is the foundation for this book.

Contemporary debates about the structure, function, design, meaning, and context of human sexual expression have presented Christians with enormous theological challenges, as the issue of homosexuality has made painfully evident. What feels like a birthright license to speak comfortably about one's innate "sexuality" is being shaken by research arguing that our sexual selves are not essentially biological or theological, with clearly demarcated boundaries symbolized by heterosexuality, but are complex formulations shaped significantly by culture and subject to change and disruption. The selfish trajectories of sexual excitement have been problematic for Christian theology since the time of Augustine. Their representations in pornography only add fuel to a longstanding struggle to determine the role that sex can play in Christian life. In the clash of angry voices about the purported evils of pornography, it has seemed especially urgent to ask about its redemptive possibilities—and even to venture as a statement of faith that (in the poet Theodore Roethke's words) "the spirit knows the flesh it must consume."

Acknowledgements

I wish to thank the following individuals who have provided me with significant help in completing this project:

David Miller, my research director at Syracuse University, respected the integrity of this project, encouraged me to follow my ideas wherever they led, and read the manuscript carefully. I could not have asked for a finer mentor.

Charles Winquist, teacher and friend, encouraged me along the way, reminding me on numerous occasions that this work was important and worth pursuing.

Kay Wiggins, another of my readers, pressed me to see that violence against women is a serious and present danger in our society.

Joyce Hardyman, my colleague at Lees College, read the manuscript and improved the quality of the prose on virtually every page.

Janet Lowdermilk did the typesetting, assuring me cheerfully that the job was really manageable.

Elkatawa, Kentucky, 1994

Introduction

The June 14, 1989 issue of *The Chronicle of Higher Education* featured an article by Karen J. Winkler entitled "Research on Pornography Gains Respectability, Increased Importance Among Scholars." In her review of the scholarship, the author noted a feminist impetus for making pornography a serious academic concern. Winkler's article incorporated remarks by a number of scholars actively studying pornography in areas such as history, literature, the behavioral sciences, and legal theory. Conspicuously absent from the article was any mention of research on pornography by scholars in religious studies. Although arguably "all restrictions that now apply to sexual behavior in Western societies stem from moral convictions enshrined in medieval canonical jurisprudence" (Brundage 1987, 587), relatively little detailed scholarly attention seems to have been paid by pornography researchers to the constraining role of Christian sexual moralities in the management of sexual representations and fantasies.

An exception to the lack of research on pornography by scholars in religious studies is Mary Jo Weaver's essay, "Pornography and the Religious Imagination," collected in *For Adult Users Only: The Dilemma of Violent Pornography*, edited by Susan Gubar and Joan Hoff (1989). Weaver's essay uses biblical, historical and contemporary materials (e.g., The Song of Songs, medieval Catholicism, and Jimmy Swaggart) to make the case that the linking of pornography to Christianity ("antipornography feminists and right-wing evangelicals

joining hands to defeat a common enemy" [68]) "does not rest with
Christian teachings about sex but with traditional Christian teaching
about women as inherently inferior" (69-70). Weaver's assertion that
Christian tradition from the Patristic period onward is "full of scorn for
women" (70) is echoed in a *Christian Century* article by scholar of
religion Mary Ellen Ross who contended that many Christian thinkers
(like pornographers) have "contempt" for women and for "human
physicality" (1990, 246).

Despite the analyses of feminists Weaver and Ross, "scorn" and
"contempt" for women does not adequately explain a man's interest in
pornography. The matter is more complicated than such terms imply.
These terms, unambiguous in their negative valence, fail to identify, for
example, the obsessional dynamics of men's interests in women's
bodies. Feminism has not done justice to the dark power that sex is
(Paglia 1990, 3), and pornography cannot be analyzed or critiqued
helpfully unless one takes seriously this dark side.

Women's bodies were a central temptation in the fantasy lives
of male ascetics (Miles 1989, 75). One wonders whether patristic
theologian Gregory of Nazianzus might have had his own monastic
experience in mind when he wrote of "the unlovely loves of the soul for
lovely bodies" (1894, 288). That men throughout the centuries of the
Christian era—celibate or otherwise—have continued to find their
fantasy lives troubled (or enlivened) by what they take to be tempting
images of women's bodies suggests that a contemporary feminist effort
to read pornography (fantasy made manifest) as a univocal expression of
men's scorn, contempt, or even hatred for women is, as an explanation,
less than complete.

This work argues that twentieth century American cultural
objections (both secular and religious) to the transgressive sexual
images of pornography are constituted, knowingly or unknowingly, by
a traditional theological construction of the sexual imagination,
recapitulated in the psychoanalytic work of Robert J. Stoller (see
below), which makes sexual excitement of any kind morally
problematic. What appears to be particularly problematic in the
contemporary literature is (illicit) sexual excitement, and the
concomitant mental imagery or fantasy, which threatens to separate sex
from love. Specifically, contemporary (the last two decades) Christian
and feminist objections to pornography manifest a latent prohibition of
imagination which is common to classical Christian perspectives

concerning the body. These objections threaten to diminish or domesticate sexual excitement by authorizing or making politically or morally appropriate only a loving or humanistic sexuality in which transgressive fantasies or images can play no part.

Psychoanalyst Robert J. Stoller's controversial argument that love plays a minimal role in sexual excitement makes salient the connection between the traditional theological materials and contemporary culture. His work captures for the contemporary cultural conversation about pornography the (Augustinian) Christian suspicion that sexual excitement, and particularly inordinate sexual excitement, is destructive, disrespectful, and hurtful, and can be allowed to play only a minimal role in any romantic or spiritual economy. As Stoller himself puts it: "My theory makes sexual excitement just one more example of what others have said for millennia: that humans are not a very loving species—especially when they make love" (1979b, 35).

Outline

Chapter 1 locates pornography on the contemporary cultural landscape. Heightened social concern about both domestic violence and sexual abuse has led frequently to indictments of pornography for its alleged contribution to the decline of civility and respect—especially toward women. Videocassette technology has meant that adults curious about pornographic movies can now watch them in the privacy of their homes—and many do. There appears to be a gap between the frequent public condemnations of pornography, on the one hand, and evidence that X-rated videos are a popular choice among many adults, female as well as male, on the other. One attempt to bridge this gap between the ideological and the personal has been the effort to distinguish acceptable sexual materials (erotica) from unacceptable ones (pornography). This chapter takes a close look at how American feminists have tried to negotiate this distinction.

Chapter 2 attempts to situate the problematic of pornography in a context of sexual liberalism decisively informed by the research studies of William H. Masters and Virginia E. Johnson, which began appearing in 1966. Until feminists argued that many sexually explicit materials were constructed to serve a man's pleasure and not a woman's, the question of what to do about pornography appeared to be a fairly straightforward clash between sexual liberals, on the one side, and sexual conservatives, on the other. The agenda of sex therapists and other advocates of liberal sexual culture was an unabashed advocacy of genital satisfactions, especially orgasm, and their work was widely perceived as providing an egalitarian model for heterosexual relationships: the woman's orgasm was every bit as important as the man's. Pornographic materials could take their place in a therapeutic or personal growth program that offered both masturbation and the cultivation of sexual fantasies as part and parcel of healthy sexual expression.

Chapter 3 can be construed as an effort to examine what went wrong with liberal sexual culture in America. Not only has the paradigmatic work of Masters and Johnson begun to break down under the often relentless criticisms of those feminists who decry its perceived "heterosexist" bias, but the issue of pornography has managed to polarize the contemporary feminist movement in North America over the question of how various expressions of human sexuality are to be understood and assessed. A central purpose of this chapter, which explores what (predominantly) American feminists have said about issues such as sexual objectification, power, fantasy, masturbation, and genital sex, is to establish the clear lack of unanimity among feminists regarding pornography. A careful examination of the feminist literature fails to support any easy moral or political consensus that pornography is always and everywhere offensive to women.

Chapter 4 argues that Christian understandings of sexual practice hold the key to comprehending much of the furor about pornography in North America. Christian theological reflection on sexuality, from patristic, medieval, and twentieth century perspectives, has displayed a decided discomfort with the human capacity to imagine sexual scenarios. In the ascetical vocations of both marriage and celibacy, sexual images—intrapsychic fantasies and the more public pornographies—are a temptation to relational infidelity. Contemporary Christian objections to pornography, from both Roman Catholic and Protestant directions, are typically buttressed by restrictions on, if not rejections of, sexual fantasy. The chapter concludes by demonstrating that Christian and feminist objections to pornography appear to be homologous in their attempts to restrict, confine, or denature the productions of the sexual imagination in the service of sexuality that is egalitarian (if not necessarily monogamous for some feminists).

Chapter 5 presents and discusses psychoanalyst Robert J. Stoller's thesis that hostility plays a major role in generating sexual excitement. Stoller has argued controversially that for most individuals, and not just for the perverted or sexually unusual, sexual excitement is produced far less often by love and affection than by mechanisms of revenge and degradation. According to this view, dehumanizing and fetishistic images—the images of pornography—are seen to be an integral part of the erotic fantasy lives of normal as well as clinically perverse individuals. Stoller's thesis that love plays a minimal role in sexual excitement may terminally complicate any attempt to distinguish acceptable sexual materials (erotica) from unacceptable ones (pornography). And yet, in returning vitality and power to sexual excitement, Stoller has reprised an old theological argument whose respect for the unruly force of sexual desire was unmistakable.

Chapter 6 argues that a feminist theological perspective invested in the relational possibilities of sex cannot measure the spiritual dimensions of pornography because pornography is used primarily in solitary sexual activity. A more promising alternative is a Jungian reading of pornography as a manifestation of the shadow side of the human personality whose redemptive power requires a willingness to embrace the perverted images of the psyche. Pornography is disturbing primarily because it subverts the communicative possibilities of sex, reminding its users that desire is a profligate and faithless master. Although not fully redeemable in a value system that treasures fidelity and monogamy, pornography is, nevertheless, spiritually redemptive—rich contemporary testimony that amidst hostilities which divide them, women and men are exploring deep longings for sexual satisfaction.

Chapter 1

The Problematic Place of Pornography in Culture

The dilemma of pornography is squarely in the mainstream of American life. The highly visible and rhetorically effective opposition on the part of feminism and Christianity alike has established a perception in the public domain that the extremities and transgressions of pornography are not, and must not be, aspects of the sexual practice of proper women and faithful Christians. Further, on this view, any individual who confesses to an interest in pornography is seen to be the enemy of decent people everywhere. It is important to the argument of this study that the dilemma of pornography be returned to those who have disowned it in the name of a purified, even docetic, agenda for sexual practice.

The availability of X-rated videocassettes for viewing in the privacy of the home, along with their enormous popularity, threatens to undo a conviction that feminists and Christians are not in fact interested in pornography—or possibly suggests that for those feminists and Christians, and others, who are politically opposed to pornography there may be a hypocritical gap between public policies and private pleasures, between ideology and practice. Further, the considerable interest in prurient sexuality in America—pornographic videos, but also sexually explicit magazines, phone sex, live sex shows, and erotically focused media advertising—fuels the suspicion that neither Christians

1

nor feminists opposed to pornography really speak to, or for, a sizeable portion of actual sexual culture in this country.

Contemporary American feminists have written much about the purported differences between pornography and erotica. If women's sexual pleasure is taken seriously, much of the pornography that has been produced almost exclusively for men must seem physically, and doubtless emotionally, stunted and one-sided to women. Can there be a pornography for women, which presents the graphic details of sexual excitement from a woman's perspective, or is there something about the genre of pornography that makes it an inappropriate vehicle for the expression of women's sexual pleasures? If pornography is inherently degrading and victimizing, can an approved form of sexual representation—erotica—be promoted which does justice to the complexities of sexual desire but does not make women, or men, into sex objects or otherwise indignify them? Further, can a collection of sexually explicit materials be identified that is robust and vigorous in its carnality but also pure? Or, finally, must the effort to cull the erotic and cast out the pornographic come to grief over the unruly demands of the body in heat?

The Dilemma of Pornography

Public sentiment about pornography is perhaps more negative now, in the mid-1990s, than at any other time in the last two decades. Revelations of the extent of domestic violence and sexual abuse in America have acted to temper any easy enthusiasm for varieties of sexual expression that appear to cause harm to others, including the perceived harm of assault on human dignity. Along with grave concern about domestic violence and sexual abuse has come a fresh challenge to the adequacy of the liberal model of free sexual expression between consenting adults. Can the umbrella of "consenting adults" cover sexual behavior deemed to be violent or abusive? Though it is not clear how, or by whom, these determinations of harm might be made, sexual practices of many types, and their representations in sexually explicit or suggestive literature and film, are being called into question by Americans who are both distraught over the increase in domestic violence and sexual abuse and concerned about the role that media expression may play in creating harmful attitudes and behaviors in homes and communities.

With the advent of men's magazines such as *Playboy*, sexually explicit materials were granted status, grudgingly at times, on the margins of decent society: the material representations of an acknowledged, long-standing male interest in female nudity. This liberalization by public consensus of sexual culture in America perhaps reached its symbolic zenith in 1970 in the presidential *Report of the Commission on Obscenity and Pornography*. This group recommended that "federal, state, and local legislation prohibiting the sale, exhibition, or distribution of sexual materials to consenting adults should be repealed." It noted that many American adults sought out sexually explicit materials as a source of entertainment and information and that the use of these materials had not been shown to lead to sexual activity other than that "already established as usual activity for the particular individual" (57-59).

However, by the time of the *Final Report of the Attorney General's Commission on Pornography*, in 1986, and amidst growing evidence of the erosion of traditional family life and values, numbers of Americans were persuaded that liberal culture had gone too far in matters of sexual expression. A tolerance in the 1970s for explicit sexual materials was out of place in a decade whose sexually explicit materials were believed to reflect all too graphically the culture's own excesses of violence and abuse. Although the 1986 commissioners recommended enforcement of existing obscenity laws rather than any new efforts at censorship (77-83), it was clear to them that the pornography of 1986 was not the pornography of 1970. The commission concluded that "the available evidence strongly supports the hypothesis that substantial exposure to sexually violent materials as described here bears a causal relationship to antisocial acts of sexual violence and, for some subgroups, possibly to unlawful acts of sexual violence" (40).

However, respected behavioral scientists, among them Edward Donnerstein, Daniel Linz and Steven Penrod, have registered substantial disagreement with the pronouncements of the Meese Commission. In *The Question of Pornography: Research Findings and Policy Implications*, they dispute claims that there is more violence in pornography today than there was in 1970 (1987, 88-91). Further, they contend that "the violence against women in some types of R-rated films shown in neighborhood theaters and on cable TV far exceeds that portrayed in even the most graphic pornography" (ix). Thus, unless all sexual representation is by definition somehow violent, discussions of pornography which conflate sex and violence obscure the question of how these two discrete cues may function to arouse individuals. For example, research suggests that to the degree that sadistic rapists are drawn to pornography, "they are attracted not by the sexual explicitness of the material but by the violent nature of some pornographic depictions" (70). While the Meese Commission report, with its emphasis on violent pornography, found a largely sympathetic audience among the many Americans concerned about the quality of family and community life, it failed to confront adequately the fact that pornography is consumed willingly by millions of single and married Americans who find that it facilitates sexual arousal and provides sexual excitement.

The 1970 presidential commission had noted that "of all the presumed consequences of exposure to erotic stimuli, the effect of sexual excitement is probably the most widely held and commonly mentioned" (198). By 1986, however, although evidence showed an enormous viewer market for pornographic materials, questions of sexual excitement had virtually disappeared from discussions of pornography in public forums, replaced primarily by concerns about pornography's role as a harm to women and a danger to family life. Were questions of sexual excitement off limits? Was all sexually explicit material "degrading in and of itself," as Meese Commissioner James Dobson believed (*Final Report* xx), or did the significant interest in pornography among many Americans signal a major discrepancy between public and private moralities?

How interested are Americans in pornography? Based on information available to it, the Meese Commission reported that as many as half of the general video retailers in the country carry cassettes that would commonly be considered pornographic (*Final Report*, 28). In the fall of 1987, Morality in Media, in its *Report on the Multi-Billion Dollar Traffic in Pornography*, estimated that over 41 million U.S. householders owned videocassette recorders, that 104 million X-rated videos were rented in 1986 alone, and that "the combined profits from both the sale and rental of pornographic videocassettes is now approaching the $1 billion mark" (7).

Are men the only ones watching these films? In a speech originally delivered in 1978, ardent antipornography feminist Andrea Dworkin claimed that "since women do not consume pornography, women cannot boycott it by not buying it" (1980, 258). And in the prologue to her 1981 book *Pornography and Silence*, Susan Griffin wrote: "a woman's mind ought to be surprised by pornography, for most women do not read pornography. We do not even enter those places or neighborhoods where it is sold" (3).

Recent information suggests that a different assessment of women's use of pornography is in order. In particular, the advent in the 1980s of sexually explicit materials produced by and for women suggests a degree of female interest not hitherto experienced or explored. Also, a 1987 survey of twenty-six thousand readers of *Redbook* magazine found that "nearly half the women surveyed say they regularly watch pornographic films, and 85 percent say they have seen at least one such film, as opposed to 60 percent in 1974" (in Williams 1989, 231). If watching pornography merits any particular political or moral scrutiny, evidence suggests that numbers of women must be included along with the men who have been presumed to make up the bulk of the audience for sexually explicit materials.

But what if the commercial success of pornography is read not primarily as a sign of moral decay but rather as a confession of sexual pleasure? Surely it would be simplistic to hold technology accountable for having created a problem of sexual prurience hitherto unknown to generations of American men and women. Doubtless, for more than a few Americans the spread of videocassette recorders and the availability of X-rated cassettes in many neighborhood video stores—in short, the opportunity to watch explicit sexual movies in the privacy of the home—will test the fit between public and private judgment on the subject of pornography.

Except for individuals radically opposed to any sexually explicit or even sexually suggestive material, discussions purporting to be about pornography often lead to questions of whether there is not some other grade or type of material that offers an affirmable representation of human sexuality—"erotic" material which stimulates the sexual appetite but does so without representing women and men in ways that are violent, degrading or demeaning. No aspect of the pornography controversy has been more frustrating than this one.

Despite noting that to "call something 'pornographic' is plainly, in modern usage, to condemn it" (7), the 1986 Meese Commission *Final Report* recognized that "erotica" is often used to reflect a judgment rather than a definition, that is, "to describe sexually explicit materials of which the user of the term approves" (8). Thus, they chose instead to attempt the use of "pornography" as a descriptive rather than condemnatory term, and intended it to mean "only that the material is predominantly sexually explicit and intended primarily for the purpose of sexual arousal" (7).

Along with many other groups studying pornography, the Meese Commission recognized that not all sexually explicit material could be lumped together into one catch-all category; consequently, they proposed to treat pornography according to an organizational schema which separated out three distinct classes of sexually explicit materials: violent, degrading, and mutual. As the commissioners discovered, this was a difficult schema to follow, particularly in determining what was to count as "degrading" (1986, 43).

Despite their major concern with questions of violence, and their professed belief that sexually violent pornography was on the increase (1986, 39), the commissioners gave significant attention to the category of "degrading but non-violent" materials, noting that these constitute "somewhere between the predominant and the overwhelming portion of what is currently standard fare heterosexual pornography . . ." (42). The Commission results do not lend much support to an ideological hope that there exists a current catalogue of sexually explicit erotica that meets any consensual judgment as to what mutually satisfying sex between equals should look like. In fact, the commissioners could not identify even one film that fit their designation of material that was both non-violent and non-degrading (1986, xx).

In the wake of the commission's Report, any attempt to define a form of sexual representation that is neither offensive, because explicit, nor harmful, because violent or degrading, appears to promise little in the way of satisfaction. What is to count as offensive or harmful seems always to entail normative considerations whose measurements will vary from individual to individual and from community to community.

Feminist Efforts to Define Erotica

Discussions of pornography have been complicated by a feminist political agenda for which pornography exemplifies illegitimate (male) power rather than representing particular, and conceivably desirable, kinds of sexual activity. Militant feminists such as Andrea Dworkin do not support a liberal critical agenda that would offer men and women some aesthetic criteria for distinguishing the pornographic from the erotic. In the preface to her 1981 *Pornography: Men Possessing Women*, Dworkin makes it clear that in her view erotica exists in a male system of power and is "simply high-class pornography."

It may be that pornography does not function in a woman's sexual economy as it functions in a man's, where it is used to achieve or enhance sexual arousal followed by masturbation. Writing about female responses to sexual material from a psychological perspective, Christine Pickard reviewed research findings that "tend to support the idea that the female experience of sexual arousal is not specifically genital, as a function of masturbation, as it seems to be in the male" (1982, 107). Or it may be the case, as a number of researchers have pointed out, that until recently masturbation and fantasy, arguably important for achieving healthy sexual functioning, have been socially disapproved for most women. In "Masturbation and Women's Sexuality," Jacqueline Fortunata critiqued Western culture's male theories of sexuality which "are biased in favor of . . . sex with a partner" (1980, 389) and concluded: "perhaps few men can appreciate the fact that masturbation is an important means of independence and self-reliance for women" (407).

Noted feminist writer Robin Morgan has claimed that most women do not find pornography arousing but, instead, "seem to be more aroused by subjects involving 'romance,' itself a metaphor for emotional contact, affection, passion, tenderness, in other words *relationships* between persons, not mere organs" (1978, 55). However, according to psychological researcher Julia Heiman: "explicit sex, not romance, is what turns people on—women as well as men" (1975, 92).

The politicizing of sexuality has meant that feminists have found themselves at odds not only with an individualistic culture unaccustomed to thinking that sex in private was anyone else's business but also with sex researchers—a group often taken to be supportive of women's sexual agendas. In *Becoming Orgasmic: A Sexual and Personal Growth Program for Women*, originally published in 1976, researchers Julia Heiman and Joseph LoPiccolo, in a section on the role of sexual fantasy, distinguished the terms erotica and pornography and noted that some ("hard-core, sex-for-sex's-sake") pornography might be offensive to women, but stated categorically: "all pornography is about sex" (1988, 81). Almost the opposite position about the relation of pornography to sex has been maintained by feminist Lorenne Clark in "Liberalism and Pornography." There Clark claimed unequivocally: "pornography has very little to do with sex . . . but it has everything to do with showing how to use sexuality as an instrument of active oppression, and that is why it is wrong" (1983, 53). Clark's feminist judgment that pornography, whether hard-core or soft-core, is not really about sex but about oppression not only functions to make female interest in pornographic materials problematic but also prompts curiosity about what, if anything, feminist authors will be willing to affirm in the way of sexual representation. If pornography is not about sex, is erotica about sex?

According to Gloria Steinem, erotica is rooted in passionate love and "the yearning for a particular person," whereas pornography is not about mutual love, or love at all, but rather seeks to replace "a spontaneous yearning for closeness with objectification and a voyeur." The erotic "doesn't require us to identify with a conqueror or a victim" (1978, 54). For Alice Walker erotica involves "the whole person" but pornography provides only "bits and pieces" (1978, 57). In pornography, according to Kate Millett, "sex is evil, dirty, morbid, secret, and shameful." Erotica, on the other hand, "operates out of good will" and "has a sense of humor, interplay, flirtation" (1978, 80).

Writing about the erotic as "power," black lesbian feminist Audre Lorde called pornography "a direct denial of the power of the erotic," for it suppresses "true feeling" and emphasizes "sensation without feeling" (1989, 209). In *Women, Sex, and Pornography*, Beatrice Faust wrote: "erotica combines the visual appeal of pornography with the emotional appeal of romance" (1980, 195).

A critical issue in feminist discussions of pornography and erotica has been whether the material in question degrades women, treating them as sexual objects or representing them engaged in sexual practices that might be considered humiliating.

"Yes, women can draw lines between eroticism and degradation," wrote Charlotte Bunch in *Take Back the Night: Women on Pornography*. "We do all know the distinction between eroticism, which celebrates our sexuality, and pornography, which degrades us" (1980, 93). In the same anthology, feminist social scientist Diana Russell claimed that a distinguishing characteristic of pornography was its "degrading or demeaning portrayal of human beings, especially women." Erotica, on the other hand, does not degrade or demean women, men, or children (218-19). For psychologists Margaret Jean

Intons-Peterson and Beverly Roskos-Ewoldsen erotica portrays "nonaggressive sexual activity between willing, sensitive, caring partners." Pornography, on the other hand, "presents the coercion of a less powerful person by a more powerful one." Women in particular are "degraded and demeaned" in pornography, represented as existing for "the satisfaction of male sexual desires and fantasies" (1989, 219). Joan Hoff, one of the editors of *For Adult Users Only: The Dilemma of Violent Pornography*, noted that for some feminists the objectification of women in sexually explicit material amounts to their "subordination" (1989, 28). And Eva Feder Kittay argued that pornography aroused sexual interest "because of the actual or intimated sexual illegitimacy of what is portrayed." Pornographic depictions trade on the presence of a female whose posture can be viewed as "humiliating or degrading" (1984, 152).

Much of the rhetoric of feminists and, as we will see, Christians, opposed to pornography has featured a primary emphasis on what are purported to be its degrading aspects, but there has been no consensus on what is to count as degrading. For example, according to philosopher Rosemarie Tong, in "degrading" sexual exchanges "the desires and experiences of at least one participant are not regarded by the other participant(s) as having a validity and a subjective importance *equal* to his/her/their own" (1982, 4). This search for the evenly mutual or equal aspects of sexual engagement raises questions, to be explored more completely in Chapters Four and Five, about whether the subjective insistence present in lust, sexual frenzy, or even orgasm makes these sexual experiences, and their representations, themselves acts of degradation by definition.

More concretely, a content analysis of X-rated video cassettes by psychological researchers Gloria Cowan *et al.* determined that at the end of a typical heterosexual scene the man "would withdraw his penis and ejaculate on the woman's stomach, face, breasts, or back just above the buttocks if he moved to a rear-entry position" (1988, 307). In the opinion of these researchers, the "filming of male ejaculation on the surface of the woman's body" as "the almost total portrayal of heterosexuality . . . demeans and degrades women's bodies" (309). Similarly, a 1988 Presbyterian Church study, *Pornography: Far from the Song of Songs*, stated that acts "such as a man ejaculating in a woman's face" were "clearly hostile" and had "little to do with mutual pleasure" (69). That the sexual acts described here are necessarily degrading or absent of any mutual pleasure has been axiomatic for many feminists. However, numbers of women report that they find them sexually arousing (Friday 1991, *passim*); Beatrice Faust, for example, has observed that some women and men "enjoy the silky feel of fresh semen, some enjoy the smell and some find it excites the imagination" (1980, 18).

Other feminists have suggested that if the meaning of human sexuality is a constructed relation rather than a given, sexual images cannot be said to have inherent pornographic or erotic meanings; in which case, as Mary Kay Blakely asked in a 1985 *Ms.* magazine article, "Is one woman's sexuality another woman's pornography?" (37). Although some feminists will agree with Charlotte Bunch that "we don't all like or respond to the same things sexually" (1980, 93), to like or respond to politically incorrect or degrading sexual activity is to risk condemnation and censure.

Sally O'Driscoll has suggested that the effort by some feminists to reclaim sexuality for women has led to a definition of erotica as "depictions of sex that turn women on, involve what women really want." Pornography then becomes "the ugly stuff that shows bondage, violence, rape—all the things men impose on women when they use them as sexual objects" (1981, 34). And Ellen Willis has remarked that the antipornography movement has made pornography "an all-purpose symbol of sex that is genitally-oriented, hence male, hence sadistic and violent, while invoking the concept of 'erotica' as code for sex that is gentle, romantic, relationship-oriented—in a word, feminine" (1982, 8).

In "Feminism and Sexuality in the 1980s," B. Ruby Rich confirmed that a key point in feminist debates about sexuality had always been "the exact identity of erotica, that tantalizing utopia of sexual turn-on hailed as delivering all the goods of arousal without any of the exploitation, violence, or objectification of conventional commercial porn" (1986, 538-39). But, as Rich had noted in an earlier article, dividing a bad pornography from a good eroticism "is rather like redlining a neighborhood: the 'bad' neighborhood is always the place where someone *else* lives." According to Rich, the effort to distinguish pornography from eroticism inevitably ends with the judgment, "If I like it, it's erotic; if you like it, it's pornographic" (1982, 17).

Can erotica, which purportedly expresses personhood and mutual respect, be distinguished from pornography, whose images of domination and violence are objectionable to many feminists? Or is this question really a matter of individual taste? In *Hard Core: Power, Pleasure, and the "Frenzy of the Visible,"* her exhaustive 1989 study of hard-core film pornography, Linda Williams wrote: "the pat polar oppositions of a soft, tender, nonexplicit women's erotica and a hard, cruel, graphic phallic pornography have begun to break down" (6) because "the erotic and the pornographic interact in hard core. The one emphasizes desire, the other satisfaction" (277).

In a 1979 article on Harlequin novels as a form of pornography for women, Ann Barr Snitow stressed that the attempt to separate an erotic sexuality ("a sensuality that can exist without violence") from a perverse or pornographic one ("driven, power hungry, intense, and selfish") left out "too much of what is infantile in sex—the reenactment of early feelings, the boundlessness and omnipotence of infant desire and its furious gusto." In Snitow's view, the total sexualization of everything which pornography offers can be only a fantasy for adults, "but does the fact that it cannot be actually lived mean this fantasy must be discarded?" (153). Why should sexual fantasies bear a burden of accountability we don't demand of other kinds of fantasy?

To disown the pornographic in order to purify one's politics may be to play into the hands of forces too complex for complete rational control. According to Muriel Dimen, regardless of conscious intention, the journey of sexual pleasure "is determined finally by a complex mix of conscious and unconscious, rational and irrational currents that represent a swirling together of personal desire and cultural force" (1984, 141). In a 1979 editorial in the *Village Voice*, Ellen Willis called pornography "the return of the repressed." In utopia pornography would wither away, but in the present reality "the sexual impulses that pornography appeals to are part of virtually everyone's psychology" (8).

Numbers of feminists seem willing to grant at least qualified support for a psychoanalytic perspective which recognizes that there are theoretical limits to change in the human psyche with regard to sexual desire (Williams 1989, 270). Others seemingly have refused the verdict that, short of utopia, there is always a transgressive aspect or "dark side" to erotic fantasy and have pressed on in search of a higher grade of erotica which "operates out of good will" (Millett) and "doesn't require us to identify with a conqueror or a victim" (Steinem).

Anais Nin had written erotica 50 years ago, but it was produced at a dollar a page for an unseen male collector. Reflecting years later on her experience in 1941, Nin wrote: "I was already conscious of a difference between the masculine and feminine treatment of sexual experience" (1977, xv). Without the constraint of writing for a male audience, how might women write about women's sexual experience? In a 1989 issue of *Libido*, a new journal devoted to what the editors describe as "tasteful, intelligent erotica" (5), Susie Bright remarked that because women "have had so little of women's sexual fiction, there is absolutely no formula to follow" (15).

Popular collections of women's sexual fantasies, such as those by Nancy Friday, have failed to meet some feminists' criteria that women should not enjoy, and should not be portrayed as enjoying, any sexual role where their sexual needs are subordinate to men's, where there is inordinate interest in phallic pleasures, or where women, or men, are made into victims.

But the Friday collections do not exhaust the range of women's writing about what interests them sexually. Psychologist and sex therapist Lonnie Barbach has edited two collections of erotic writing by women. *Pleasures: Women Write Erotica*, published in 1984, featured erotic writing ostensibly based on the authors' experiences and, in its discursive sections, touched upon sexual issues usually associated with the pornographic which have nevertheless found their way into women's erotic writing: the dark side of erotic fantasy, power, illicit or forbidden sex, and sexual objectification. *Erotic Interludes: Tales Told by Women*, which appeared in 1986, broadened the erotic venue to include a number of stories with no grounding in the authors' realms of experience, in recognition that fiction is more complex, with deeper levels of meaning (3).

Some female writers of erotica have been notably circumspect about what could count as acceptable sexual expression. For example, The Kensington Ladies' Erotica Society, a group of women over 40 from the San Francisco area, produced two collections of erotica (1984, 1986) which were featured in widely circulated Book of the Month Club catalogues. In the introduction to their first volume the authors, after noting their displeasure with Nancy Friday, Anais Nin, men's sexually oriented magazines (*Penthouse*, etc) and the general sexual stereotyping of women, laid down the one rule that would direct their writing of erotica: there must be no victims (1984, 4). In an afterword to the second volume one writer said, "It is the rule we Kensington Ladies live by, and I will do whatever I must to get it across" (1986, 218).

The rule regarding victimization led to some judgment calls about which of the erotic stories produced by the Kensington Ladies could merit approval by the group. One participant alluded to an "explicit" story she had produced, whose intent, she said, was "to come from real experience instead of fantasy," which the group found "too close to victimization . . . although it evidently stirred up a lot of down-and-dirty talk." In the wake of the unfavorable reception of her story, she reported: "it is only now that I can see the degree to which the 'free spirit' I thought I was has been slave to old forms and images" (1984, 223-24). Another participant expressed her impatience with the group's writing projects ("not enough *fucking*, for god's sake!") and declared that "down-and-dirty was most erotic" to her, but then acknowledged: "I learned that there can also be eroticism in atmosphere and even in humorous situations" (1984, 225).

Along with the Kensington rule that the erotic must not include any perceived victimization of women by men, or by other women, came a belief that the erotic is not primarily about localized genital sensations at all but is rather about the whole panoply of sensual experiences—where the sexually erotic is continuous, or even interchangeable, with the erotics of peeling oranges and folding fresh laundry. As one Kensington writer put it, the erotic is "smells, sounds, memories, sensations, colors, feelings, flowers, grass, sunlight, wind, rain, thoughts . . . " (1986, 211). Put another way, by editor Laura Chester in the introduction to *Deep Down*, a 1988 collection of women's erotic writings: "the focus . . . goes way beyond localized desire, leading us to a more diaphanous enticement, where sensuality penetrates every aspect of the world" (2).

A different collection of women's erotic writing, *Touching Fire*, edited by Louise Thornton, Jan Sturtevant, and Amber Coverdale Sumrall, continued the emphasis on the erotic as what connects the woman with "the life force of the universe" (1989, 5). Here, the body is "the entranceway into the spiritual" (4) and the erotic opposes the pornographic, which "robs women of the wholeness implicit in their connection with all of life" (7). As one contributor noted: "my sense of the erotic does not include the pornographic." For this woman the erotic is an awareness "of the holy in the relationship between spirit and mind and the things of this world—body, leaf, stone" (213).

For the editors of *Touching Fire*, "the erotic, neither trivialized nor degraded but allowed to be as pure and elemental as an ocean wave, is almost always sensual" (1989, 3). They dedicated the volume to black lesbian feminist Audre Lorde, whose view of the erotic they self-consciously adopted (2). Lorde had written about the erotic in a very non-genital way, opposing it to the pornographic, and blurring any assumed distinction between what is erotic and what is not: "there is, for me, no difference between writing a good poem and moving into sunlight against the body of the woman I love" (1989, 212). For the editors of *Touching Fire*, following Lorde, the erotic is "more than the sexual" and includes "finding or creating satisfying work, finding joy, allowing sorrow . . . making love or walking through clear light, opening our hearts, digging in the earth, planting" (1989, 6).

Has the effort by some women to reclaim a woman's erotica which is not primarily focused on the particularities of genital expression but which reaches out into the world to find the sensual connections everywhere, actually functioned to deny other women a believable sexual identity or to redefine so radically the erogenous zones as to remove any connection these zones may have to male or female sex organs—dispersing sexual tensions to the four winds and beyond? How credible, finally, is the statement of one of the authors in *Touching Fire*, with thoughts doubtless echoing those of Audre Lorde: "in my daily life I experience no separation between the erotic, the nonerotic" (1989, 213)?

In a review of *Weaving the Visions: New Patterns in Feminist Spirituality*, Carol LeMasters has criticized the views of Lorde and other feminist authors in that volume for seeming to deny to the area of sexuality a specificity it deserves so that they can accent a more holistic approach to feminist spirituality. According to LeMasters, "when everything is erotic, the word itself loses all meaning." It may be "that sexuality is *not* interchangeable with other sensual experiences, else our feelings about it would not be so intense nor our debates about it so bitter. Perhaps what is needed is to "reevaluate our complex feelings about *sex as sex*" (1989, 16).

Chapter 2

Sexual Liberalism in America

One of the defining characteristics of pornographic materials is their intent to arouse the reader or viewer sexually. Once aroused through pornography, the individual typically seeks release, satisfaction, or completion of the physiological cycle through orgasm. Though pornographic or sexually explicit materials appear to have found significant acceptance among women and couples, their traditional market has been the masturbating male, for whom they provide an immediate environment of sexual stimulation and a temporarily enhanced repertoire of sexual fantasy images or memories.

Pornography has been deemed objectionable in large measure because it disengages the physiology and fantasy of sex from the relational aspects of sex, suggesting that sexual excitement is an intensely personal and even idiosyncratic matter whose dimensions are not contained by personal loyalty to significant others. The very presence of pornography suggests that sexual excitement is by nature wayward and self-seeking. Intense individual orgasms, generated by masturbation and often accompanied by fantasy-images of sexual partners and practices whose lure may be beyond the pale of a particular commitment to sexual monogamy, challenge a traditional understanding of sexual practice whose presumed focus is the couple.

The last twenty-five years in America have seen the advance, and perhaps partial retreat, of a wide liberal culture of orgasm and genital satisfaction which has focused on the rights of individuals, particularly women, to pleasure in sexual activity. The well-known studies of sex researchers and therapists William Masters and Virginia Johnson, which began appearing in 1966, are emblematic of this culture. Masturbation and sexual fantasy, and their implied challenge to the sexual couple as the assumed focus of therapeutic intervention, have figured prominantly in a clinical program for sexual satisfaction whose appeal has extended beyond the frame of sex therapy and become part of the personal agenda and self-understanding of numbers of individuals in the society at large.

In a sexually charged culture the physiological intensities of sexual experience are coveted regardless of whether they are achieved in relation with actual sexual partners.

Sexual Physiology

A distinguishing feature of the Masters and Johnson's approach to human sexuality has been its emphasis on sexual anatomy and physiology. Between 1954 and 1965 William Masters and Virginia Johnson observed more than 10,000 episodes of sexual activity in a laboratory setting. Their report of these observations was published in 1966 as *Human Sexual Response*. Among their findings was the observation that, at least for women, masturbation produced a more intense orgasmic response than coitus (133). As historian Paul Robinson noted in *The Modernization of Sex*, Masters and Johnson did not claim that more intense necessarily meant more satisfying. However, "as far as the brute physiological facts are concerned, masturbation is the winner" (1989, 143).

In *Human Sexual Inadequacy*, published in 1970, Masters and Johnson coined the diagnostic term "masturbatory orgasmic inadequacy" to address the difficulties of the few women who were able to reach orgasm through coitus but not through self-manipulation. For Robinson, this translation of the unsuccessful pursuit of masturbation into a pathological condition represented "the most extravagant assertion of the modernist theory of masturbation" (1989, 144). Although this celebration of masturbation could be read as liberating women from their sexual dependency on men (142), it also seemed to make masturbation "the ultimate criterion of sexual behavior" (13).

By the 1980s Masters and Johnson appeared to have backed away from the implication that the person who does not masturbate is somehow sexually dysfunctional. In *Masters and Johnson on Sex and Human Loving*, co-authored in 1982 with Robert C. Kolodny and reprinted several times, the writers say, perhaps in self-criticism: "in the rush to legitimize masturbation, there is often a built-in implication that everyone *should* masturbate." Personal decisions not to masturbate, sometimes made for religious reasons, need to be respected. "People who have *never* masturbated, while in a statistical minority, should certainly not be made to feel abnormal" (1988, 297). Despite this *mea culpa* regarding certain excesses of what Robinson had dubbed "the modernist dogma of masturbation's innocence" (1989, 145), Masters and Johnson continued to challenge the individual to take responsibility for his or her own sensual and sexual pleasure. It was a mistake, they said, to expect the other to provide one with "joyful paroxysms of sexual pleasure." For, in actuality, "we are each responsible for our own eroticism" (453).

If masturbation is no longer the *sine qua non* of healthy sexual functioning in the Masters and Johnson paradigm, has its chastening really diminished its appeal? Those women who preferred coital orgasms to masturbatory ones "often say that the overall experience is more satisfying, but the actual orgasm is less direct and intense" (1988, 73). To be sure, intensity of sexual experience does not always spell satisfaction or meaning, but intensity of any kind of experience registers its own declaration and requires its own kind of acknowledgement. The intensity of the masturbatory orgasm would seem to be no exception.

Numbers of clinicians and researchers in the last twenty years appeared to accept as foundational the Masters and Johnson emphasis on the anatomy and physiology of sexual expression—the subjectively reported or objectively recorded intensities of discrete sexual acts. In particular, these clinicians and researchers witnessed widely to the value of masturbation as valid sexual experience. Not only was masturbation believed to be a way to secure a physiological basis for heterosexual pleasures, it was also a confession of a particular degree of orgasmic intensity, with or without relational entailments.

The focus on masturbation was not something new with Masters and Johnson. In his 1953 study, *Sexual Behavior in the Human Female*, Kinsey had noted: "pre-marital experience in masturbation may actually contribute to the female's capacity to respond in her coital relations in marriage" (172). He observed that masturbation was the type of sexual activity "in which the female most frequently reaches orgasm" (132). Perhaps it should come as no surprise, then, that a generation subsequent to Kinsey's, with its raised consciousness regarding women's sexual enjoyment, would advance masturbation as a sexual activity meaningful on its own terms and not useful solely as a preliminary to heterosexual connections.

Contemporary paeans to the benefits of masturbation are plentiful. A 1977 study of women's sexual fantasies, by psychologist Karen Shanor, called masturbation the "gateway to sexuality" and suggested that a woman's decision to masturbate may mean "she is taking a large step toward accepting and enjoying her own sexuality" (33). For Betty Dodson, in *Sex For One*, "masturbation is . . . the best way to gain sexual self-knowledge and to let go of old sexual fears and inhibitions" (1987, 4). In their 1988 book, *Becoming Orgasmic*, Julia Heiman and Joseph LoPiccolo, after highlighting the Masters and Johnson research on the strength and intensity of masturbatory orgasms, went on to note that a less obvious value of masturbation is its emphasis that "*your body belongs first of all to you.*" "In fact, if your body belongs to your partner, so will your pleasure, your pain, your arousal, and eventually your orgasms" (56).

Following the laboratory work of Masters and Johnson, researchers and therapists alike have had to confront, and determine the significance of, the physiological and psychological intensity of masturbation. Nevertheless, the physiological truth of the masturbatory orgasm has not gone unchallenged. What Robinson had viewed as the modernist belief in masturbation's innocence (1989, 145) has not found uniform subscription among sex researchers and therapists, especially in the 1980s.

Researchers have disputed the claims of those who advocate masturbation as a helpful means of becoming orgasmic with a partner. For example, one researcher found misleading the claim that learning to masturbate, first alone and then in the presence of one's partner, was frequently "a transitional step to being stimulated to orgasm by the partner . . . " (Wakefield 1987, 13). Another cited the case of a woman whose sexual preference for intercourse over masturbation was called into question by a woman therapist who told her that this preference indicated too much dependency on men and not enough enjoyment of her own clitoris (Ellison 1984, 328). Writing about the particular needs of lesbian clients, JoAnn Loulan affirmed the value of masturbation exercises as a means of teaching women about their orgasmic response (1988, 229) but drew attention to the presence in our culture of a "tyranny of orgasm" approach in which orgasmic response has become the arbiter of what is to count as fulfilling sex (228).

In light of these criticisms, the witness of masturbation to a degree of orgasmic intensity unmatched for many by the orgasmic intensity of coitus seems in danger of becoming a testimony only to narcissism and misdirected sexual focus. Should the goal of sex be so starkly focused on orgasm? A feminist therapeutic approach to sex has held that sexual satisfaction is related more to emotional factors than to smooth performance, and that if therapy is indicated, it might be useful as "treatment for politically incorrect relationships" rather than to confirm clients in a normative expectation that orgasm is the necessary sign of satisfaction (Tiefer 1988).

The question of what to do about the brute physiological facts of the orgasmic intensity of masturbation is only temporarily displaced by a revisionist strategy for sex therapy now invested in more of the relational aspects of human sexual expression. This revisionist strategy was symbolized by the expansion of a popular orgasmic growth program for women, first published in 1976, whose formulation was extended in 1988 to convey "a broader focus than just reaching orgasm" (Heiman and LoPiccolo xi). Nevertheless, the question of the measurement of raw sexual excitement—with or without the presence of a sex partner—remains, and is germane to the role of fantasy in sexual arousal.

Sexual Fantasy

The Kinsey studies of male and female sexual behavior found that for those who masturbated, 72 percent of the males and 50 percent of the females almost always used fantasies (1953, 667). Studies since Kinsey have continued to demonstrate the presence of masturbatory fantasy among various populations, and a positive connection between masturbation and the use of fantasies has been taken for granted by many sex researchers and therapists. According to Masters and Johnson, sexual fantasies "are often combined with masturbation to provide a source of turn-on when a partner is not available . . . " (1988, 269). Researchers have observed that inorgasmic women often have little or no sexual fantasy life (Goleman and Bush 1977, 104), and therapists have offered women seeking greater orgasmic satisfaction specific suggestions for expanding their ability to fantasize (Heiman and LoPiccolo 1988, 83).

Nevertheless, the connection between sexual fantasy and the practice of masturbation has not been without its perceived dangers. In his 1984 *Education of the Senses*, historian Peter Gay quoted one of the great pedagogues of the eighteenth century who classed masturbation as undesirable because it would "fill the imagination with revolting and tormenting pictures" and "ruin all hopes of a happy marriage" (308). Thus, well in advance of a media age with its visual technologies, sexual fantasy had been fingered as a dangerous indulgence.

What about fantasy during sexual relations with another person? Here there has been perhaps even more disagreement among sex therapists and researchers than on the therapeutic effectiveness of masturbation. Products of the sexual imagination can be extremely powerful and, whether generated by a masturbatory impulse or not, might function to estrange lovers by providing an intervening mental stimulation whose effect is arguably to take something intangible, but nevertheless vital, from the sexual interaction at hand.

Those with trouble affirming a positive role for sexual fantasy have turned to Sigmund Freud for support. In an essay on "Creative Writers and Day-Dreaming" Freud remarked that "a happy person never phantasies [*sic*], only an unsatisfied one. The motive forces of phantasies are unsatisfied wishes . . . " (1959, 146). In a 1971 debate with fellow psychiatrist Harold Greenwald on the role of fantasy in sexual relations, Natalie Shainess claimed that an individual who conjures up sexual images while engaging in sexual activity with a partner is in trouble. If the present relationship is unsatisfactory, she asked, why isn't the individual "off trying to meet someone else with whom he could in reality duplicate the fantasy" (50)? Shainess seemed to suggest that it might be possible, in a monogamous relationship, for reality to match fantasy, leaving the sex partners with no unsatisfied wishes.

Shainess has not been the only psychiatric researcher to take a dim view of the role of fantasy in relational sex. In a 1963 study, "Women's Fantasies During Sexual Intercourse," Marc Hollender viewed the use of fantasy by a woman during sexual relations as a means of withdrawing psychologically from both the act and the person, in part to cope with feelings of guilt (87). To Hollender, the use of fantasy meant that "in a physical and social sense, the woman is having sexual intercourse, but in an intrapsychic sense she is engaging in masturbation" (89).

Even without Hollender's judgment that use of fantasy in partner sex amounts to masturbation, the relationship of fantasy to both masturbation and partner sex raises questions of guilt and betrayal. One of the respondents in a study of women's sexual fantasies noted that during masturbation she often thought of men other than her husband: "It was 'wrong' to think of them when with him, which probably accounts for my not enjoying him" (Shanor 1977, 26).

Unbridled interest in sexual fantasies has been credited with shifting sexual activity away from coitus and toward other practices which may promise a greater degree of stimulation—a move that potentially provokes anxiety or guilt for those who believe that vaginal intercourse between married individuals defines normative sexual activity.

Christian commentator Lewis B. Smedes could have been speaking for a portion of the therapeutic as well as the religious community when he remarked that, given the world we live in: "any person who insists on being the only sexual stimulus in the world for his/her spouse is courting disillusionment" (1976, 212). But for many individuals, whether in the name of psychology or morality, fantasy has continued to symbolize a kind of unfaithfulness.

Sex therapist Jack Annon recounted the case of a 25-year-old married woman who came to him for counseling. She was anxious and upset because she had spoken casually with a man at a party and then had caught herself wondering what he would be like in bed. The client felt sinful about this fantasy and rebuffed her husband's attempts later that night to approach her sexually. Annon reported that this woman felt she had been unfaithful: "For her the thought was equal to the deed . . . ." Therapeutic help enabled her to appreciate that fantasies like these were normal and not unusual, but "she had a difficult time in 'believing' that they were relatively harmless" (1976, 51).

Disputes about the role of fantasy in sexual arousal, whether in masturbation or during sexual activity with a partner, often engage the issue of pornography. Although recent feminist debate about the sexual representation of women in our contemporary culture has targeted pornography as a prime example of how women should not be portrayed, sex therapists, until recently, have not been particularly opposed to the use of pornography by clients attempting to increase their sexual pleasure. Some have even recommended it heartily.

In their masturbation program for helping the anorgasmic woman, LoPiccolo and Lobitz noted that the idea of fantasizing during masturbation "does not seem to occur spontaneously to our female clients," and they recommended the use of pornographic reading material or pictures and erotic fantasies to enhance and increase arousal (1972, 168). Rational-Emotive Therapy (RET) founder Albert Ellis uses "imaging methods" as part of his approach. Male and female clients with arousal or orgasm difficulties are taught how to fantasize intensely without feeling ashamed of the fantasy material they produce. Ellis noted that the therapist may help a client to use sexual fantasy—"romantic fantasies," fantasies "mutually verbalized with their partners," and even "various kinds of 'pornographic' images" (1975, 15). And sex therapist Avodah Offit argued that some women, especially those whose sexual feelings had been destroyed, needed the forbidden stimulus of pornography. Women who were restricted, especially girls brought up in convents or otherwise influenced by orthodox religion, with its proscription of sexual affection before marriage, could profit from seeing "pictures of women having sex, pictures of men's organs that are frightening (and exciting) to see" (1981, 33).

Despite their apparent helpfulness in various forms of sex therapy, the use of pornographic materials has raised troubling questions. One rather obvious and categorical objection to pornography reflects a longstanding moral and religious discomfort with the deliberate cultivation of the sexual imagery of mental life, an uneasiness that has everything to do with the location of sexual activity exclusively in the marriage relationship. If fantasy is allowed or encouraged in remedial therapy, or even in sexual relationships that function reasonably well, has the monogamous nature of a sexual relationship been violated? In other words, how far into the realm of fantasy should the idea of monogamy extend?

Despite the perceived successes of the therapeutic culture's estimation of human sexuality, numbers of individuals, many of them religiously identified, have found the cultivation of sexual fantasy—often, though not always, in conjunction with masturbation—to be a threat to the marriage relationship. For example, in *True Sexuality*, his attempt at a biblically-integrated philosophy of sexuality, Ken Unger proposed that the fantasy required by masturbation created a "false understanding of sexual relationships" and that masturbation by unmarried individuals "can make marital adjustments more difficult" (1987, 208). Unger did concede that masturbation could be viewed as a "lesser evil" in some instances, and he cited the example of a businessman on an extended trip who "could conceivably reduce his vulnerability to temptation by masturbating while fantasizing about his wife" (208-9). According to Christian sociologist Herbert J. Miles, writing in the marriage manual *Sexual Happiness in Marriage*: to "imagine oneself having sex relations with someone other than one's spouse" amounted to "secret disloyalty." "Sexual fantasy about one's husband or wife is normal and good. With anyone else, it is a major danger signal" (1982, 152).

However, prescriptive desires for a monogamous sexual imagination run up against an anthropological assessment of the human condition in the West, largely Freudian in character, which holds that the human capacity for imaginal faithfulness is far less than many, especially Christian, individuals have hoped. If it had achieved nothing else, psychodynamically-oriented thought would be invaluable for emphasizing that there is no such thing as psychic life that is not flawed.

But perhaps more striking even than relatively predictable Christian objections to the therapeutic culture's acceptance of masturbation, sexual fantasy, and pornography have been the heated feminist disputes about these practices. In what may seem a counterintuitive move, given the intensity of the masturbatory orgasm for women, some feminists have accused the Masters and Johnson approach, with its focus on orgasm, of modeling sexual satisfaction on a male paradigm. For example, Janice M. Irvine, in *Disorders of Desire: Sex and Gender in Modern American Sexology*, noted that although Masters and Johnson's work "would seem to provide scientific legitimacy for the feminist strategy of equality and equivalency," their analysis is deceptive. "Masters and Johnson advance their claim of male-female similarity in the absence of any broader analysis of male dominance and heterosexism" (1990, 89). Feminists have also questioned whether allowances ought to be made for the extremities of (mostly male) sexual fantasy life. Do these intrapsychic images—whether made manifest or not—function to assault or transgress a public order which belongs every bit as much to women as to men? In a patriarchal society where women are routinely made objects and commodities, abnormal thoughts may be on their way to becoming abnormal deeds—or so it has been argued.

If the sexual representations of women often amount to pornographic defilement, then perhaps the wisdom of psychiatrists and sex therapists, with its hospitality toward the products of the sexual imagination, must be pre-empted. In calling for a reshaping, and not an accepting, of the sexual images of both dream world and reality, a new feminist agenda reverses the old therapeutic one. The role of sexual imagery in sexual arousal becomes primarily a political rather than an intrapsychic issue.

Chapter 3

Feminists Confront Pornography

Although the religious right has fought pornography from the perspective of a desire to return sex to a proper context in marriage, it is feminism that has cut the wider swath by making pornography an issue for religious and nonreligious women alike. By suggesting that a tolerance for pornography on the part of the (largely male) liberal culture actually expresses that group's subjugation of women, anti-pornography feminists have indicted not only pornographers themselves but also pornography consumers, male and female.

Those who would declare themselves in fundamental agreement with the feminist perspective on pornography do not realize that there is no one feminist perspective on the issue, that feminists disagree among themselves; in fact, not all feminists categorically oppose pornography. It is perhaps not surprising that the combined forces of the religious right, the mainstream religious groups eager to condemn violence and exploitation wherever they find it, and feminists opposed to pornography have created a strong impression in the American culture at large that pornography has no defenders or even tolerant critics among women. However, evidence that women are among the consumers of pornography subverts any easy consensus.

Heightened public concern about pornography in America, made manifest in the establishment of the Meese Commission in 1985, has supported the presumption that no self-respecting woman would admit

25

to any interest in sexually explicit materials whose purpose seems so clearly to be to arouse men by providing them with images of women in sexually subservient roles. Specifically, feminist authors opposed to pornography have assumed that women have, or should have, no interest in pornography.

Feminist testimonials to the foreignness of pornography for women have made it easier for often conservative Americans with no necessary loyalty to feminist agendas to presume that they could speak for all women when they categorically opposed pornography in American culture. Anthropologist Carole Vance observed the hearings of the arguably conservative Meese Commission. She concluded that this group had "co-opt[ed] the language of antipornography feminists," whose purpose had been to indict pornography for depicting or glorifying "sexist sex," for its own purpose of furthering a conservative sexual agenda whose understanding of degrading sex amounted to an objection to "sexual images show[ing] sex outside marriage." According to Vance, Commission Chairman Henry Hudson had "transmuted the term used by women's antipornography groups, 'the degradation of women,' into 'the degradation of femininity,' which conjured up visions of Victorian womanhood dragged from the pedestal" (1986, 79).

There has been no unanimity among women regarding the status of pornography, despite the claims made by antipornography feminists such as Brownmiller, Dworkin, and Griffin and by various conservative, often religious groups which are categorically opposed to pornography. Writing in the *Village Voice* in 1979, Ellen Willis admitted to having enjoyed "various pieces of pornography—some of them of the sleazy 42nd Street paperback sort—and so have most women I know" (8). In the course of her review of Andrea Dworkin's *Pornography: Men Possessing Women*, Sally O'Driscoll conceded her own ambivalence about pornography but remarked, "I have enjoyed some of it and I resent being pushed into a moral corner" (1981, 34). In a *Ms.* article in 1982, Barbara Ehrenreich, Elizabeth Hess, and Gloria Jacobs reported that the loss of a feminist consensus on pornography was related to the fact that "some women began to admit that they even enjoyed pornography" (87). Susie Bright, originator of the lesbian publication *On Our Backs*, more recently added a note of irony to the already complex and divisive issue of the relationship of feminism to pornography. Interviewed by journalists Steve Chapple and David Talbot for their 1989 *Burning Desires: Sex in America*, Bright spoke of fiction written by antipornography feminist Andrea Dworkin: "Andrea is a pornographer—and a great one . . . . I can't tell you how many women I know who masturbate to the dirty parts of her novel" (296).

In the introduction to *For Adult Users Only: The Dilemma of Violent Pornography* (1989), editors Susan Gubar and Joan Hoff suggested that of all the problems facing the women's movement, "pornography may be potentially the most divisive and debilitating since the fifty-year debate over protective legislation and the ERA, begun in the 1920s" (10). They noted that the Indiana University multidisciplinary faculty seminar on violence and pornography, which met throughout academic year 1985-1986 and produced most of the essays in this collection, failed to provide any consensus regarding pornography. Gubar and Hoff reported "a disheartening (as well as enlightening)" realization of "how little our discussions and arguments changed opinions in the course of the two semesters" (8).

In the introduction to *Take Back the Night*, Laura Lederer (1980) had announced that a feminist perspective on pornography, which sees pornography as "the ideology of a culture which promotes . . . crimes of violence against women," was being offered as an alternative to an earlier construction of the pornography debate which had pitted conservatives, whose concerns were with the immorality of pornography, against liberals, who saw pornography as part of "ever-expanding human sexuality" (19-20). Rather than solidly support a new, third perspective on pornography in line with Lederer's claim that pornography is a crime against women, feminists—even those who concede the reality of a patriarchal culture in which women are traded commodities—have been more deeply split on the issue of pornography than Lederer, Dworkin, Griffin, and other anti-pornography feminists would have us believe. In the course of responding to pornography in American culture, American feminists have argued a variety of positions on such issues as sexual objectification, power, fantasy, masturbation and genital sex. Their writings reveal division rather than consensus.

Sexual Objectification

A primary feminist argument against pornography has been that it invariably presents women's bodies as objects. In pornographic images "women are not seen as human beings but as things" (Russell and

Lederer 1980, 24). Susanne Kappeler has claimed that "turning another human being, another subject, woman, into an object is robbing her of her own subjectivity" (1986, 57). To be an object is to be less than a subject. "In pornography, the woman is portrayed . . . as inferior—a mere hunk of meat . . . " (Kittay 1984, 157). Catharine MacKinnon has argued that the sexual objectification of women is constitutive of a social order dominated by men, where "'woman' is defined by what male desire requires for arousal and satisfaction . . . " (1989, 318-19). For Andrea Dworkin, "male supremacy depends on the ability of men to view women as sexual objects . . . " (1981, 113). "Adult men are convinced and sincere in their perception of adult women in particular as objects" (49). Alix Kates Shulman pointed out that the feminists who picketed the Miss America Pageant in Atlantic City in 1968 used that event to "demonstrate how women are (degradingly) judged as sex objects" (1980, 594). But not all feminists have agreed that sexual objectification amounts to degradation.

E. Ann Kaplan cautioned that women "have (rightly) been wary of admitting the degree to which . . . pleasure comes from identifying with our own objectification" (1983, 314). Other feminists have focused on salutary aspects of the sexual objectification of both men and women. For example, Marcia Pally discussed some of the delights of being looked at, noting that when it is play and not a political condition, being an object is a requirement "for seduction and sex, and all the energy and replenishment it brings" (1985, 72). Pally's analysis of objectification also noted the power involved in being the one looked at: "Anyone who's ever been looked up and down and hopefully approached knows the feeling—the sense of dominion, of running the show" (73).

In "Bad Girls and 'Good' Politics," Lisa Orlando observed that women fear objectification because it has traditionally stood for sexual engagement that is "less-than-totally-personalized." Rather than eliminate the woman as sexual object, what is called for, according to Orlando, is the addition of woman as sexual subject. If women can be encouraged to provide their own sexual representations, then perhaps both subject and object can be retained, in a move Orlando sees as enabling women to maintain the option of "connecting and disconnecting sexuality and emotion" (1982, 17). Rosemarie Tong appeared to support Orlando's desire to give women the option, and not the requirement, of combining sexuality and emotion when she claimed that at times "the most enjoyable sexual experience may be one that is encumbered neither with the responsibilities of love nor with some of its more romanticized illusions" (1982, 3).

A more controversial defense of sexual objectification of women has come from within the pornographic film business itself. For a 1987 *Jump Cut* article, "Deep Inside Porn Stars," Annette Fuentes and Margaret Schrage interviewed six actresses who consider themselves feminists. Among them was Gloria Leonard, publisher of the men's magazine *High Society*. Responding to criticism that pornography degrades and objectifies women, Leonard announced, "[W]omen *are* sex objects. It's *okay* to be a sex object." Veronica Vera added, "It's delightful to be a sex object" (42).

Writing in *Heresies*, Paula Webster pointed out that "objectification may be a function of representation" and that no pornographic actors—male or female—have "depth" or "contours." "They are the ritual performers of the culture's sexual paradigms" (1981, 49). Nevertheless, numbers of women, and perhaps increasingly men, have found the sexual paradigms of American culture offensive—for example, the mass media images used to market consumer goods. There, as Valerie Miner has noted, the "subliminal messages start with the fragmentation of female bodies," where "the focus [is] on women's asses, the acrobatic spread of the model's legs, the mountainous regions of cleavage," all of which are extraneous to the product under consideration (1981, 49).

As Kathy Myers has observed, however, objectification may signify either "the process of fragmentation, which implies a breaking up or disabling of the physical form," or what she calls "a pleasure in the part," where what is portrayed can be understood "not as a butchering of the female form but as a celebration of its constituent elements . . . " (1982, 16). Perhaps the sexual objectification of women (and men)— including pornographic images—cannot fairly be rejected out of hand as marking a diminution of sexual expression, an offense against a higher erotic calling. As archetypal psychologist Patricia Berry has argued, pleasure has a polymorphous quality which "includes a sense of the lower, the multiple, and the incomplete." "Sexual details—a male shape of buttock, a female curve of hip—become qualities adding to the individual . . . " (1982, 45) rather than particulars that are subservient to a more important identity or unity.

Diffuse vs. Genital Sexuality

A variation of the feminist concern about making objects and
fetishes of women's bodies and body parts in pornography, and in the
media culture at large, appears when we look at feminist discussions of
the character of women's sexual experiences. Are women more diffuse
in their sexual pleasures and less genital than men?

Adrienne Rich, in her influential 1980 essay "Compulsory
Heterosexuality and Lesbian Existence," has suggested that to discover
the erotic in female terms is to find a "diffuse" kind of energy which is
"unconfined to any single part of the body or solely to the body itself . . ."
(650). Alice Echols has observed that for some feminists female
sexuality is thought to be "muted, diffuse, and interpersonally oriented,"
that women desire reciprocity and intimacy while "genitally oriented"
men desire power and orgasm (1983, 449). Well-known antipornography
feminist Robin Morgan has written that the male sexual style
emphasizes genital sexuality and objectification, whereas women's
sexuality places "greater trust in love, sensuality, humor, tenderness,
commitment" (1977, 181). Though legal scholar Catharine MacKinnon
questions what any notion of women's sexuality can mean in a
patriarchal culture which defines women's status as second class, she
writes that from a feminist perspective sexuality is a "pervasive
dimension throughout the whole of social life" rather than a "discrete
sphere of interaction or feeling or sensation or behavior . . . " (1989,
318).

Some feminists, however, have expressed concern that too much
emphasis on the diffuse or romanticized aspects of sex has worked to
dilute or disperse the erotic intensities of genital sexuality. The effort to
do justice to women's, and perhaps men's, sense that the sexual is more
than the genital may have meant that the "erotic" has been made to
cover too much territory—with a consequent loss of focus and
intensity.

How important is genital sexuality in defining what women's
sexuality can mean? According to Ann Ferguson (with Jacquelyn N.
Zita and Kathryn Pyne Addelson), "the ability to take one's own genital
sexual needs seriously is a necessary component of an egalitarian love
relation, whether it be with a man or a woman" (1981, 164).

But not all feminists would agree with Ferguson. Robin Morgan,
author of "pornography is the theory, and rape the practice," seems to

make problematic, for women as well as men, any genital sex that is not tender and nurturant when she claims that "rape exists any time sexual intercourse occurs when it has not been initiated by the woman, out of her own genuine affection and desire" (1977, 165). But Morgan's view of sex as "that most intimate, vulnerable, and tender of physical exchanges" (169) has seemed to other feminists to limit unfairly what female desire can mean. In an article questioning whether the women's movement was pro-sex, Ellen Willis suggested that women's sexual feelings have included "desires we long ago decided were too dangerous to acknowledge, even to ourselves." She said that "desire" is "the aspect of sex feminists have had the most trouble discussing" and suggested that it might be safer not to think that women's sexuality could bear any resemblance to "unfettered male lust" (1981, 36).

In another essay, "Toward a Feminist Sexual Revolution," Willis observed that disagreement among feminists regarding what women want sexually has led to the development of feminist sexual orthodoxies—"what women *really* want/ought to want/would want if they were not intimidated/bought off/brainwashed by men"—which have gained authoritative status and acted to limit women's sexual freedom (1982, 7). And Carole Vance and Ann Barr Snitow have argued that "hastily erected new prescriptions" about sexuality may function to heighten shame about sex, leading women to hesitate to admit "deviations" or to wonder whether what they are, or are not, doing sexually is "pathetic and sick" (1984, 134-35).

Politically correct sex for some feminists has meant what Susan Griffin called "the capacity of the female self, of a female self, to love the female self, in *oneself or in another*" (1981, 224). To others, such as philosopher Eva Feder Kittay, it has meant relations of equality, "the mutual and reciprocal giving and receiving of sexual pleasure, such that the other's desire and pleasure are constitutive of our own" (1984, 172).

Other feminists have found that too restrictive a definition of what can count as legitimate sexual expression for a woman can lead to rejecting as violent all sexuality "that doesn't meet their stringent standards of 'correctness'" (Orlando 1982, 17). In a discussion with fellow feminists Deirdre English and Amber Hollibaugh, Gayle Rubin observed that the women's movement had created a new standard about appropriate sexual conduct which is "like the old psychiatric concept, that dictates a 'normal' way to do it," and involves a restricted view of sex which is not focused on orgasm, is gentle, and "takes place in the

Feminists Confront Pornography

context of a long-term, caring relationship." Rubin called this new, legitimate feminist sex "the missionary position of the women's movement" (1981, 50).

Kittay has attempted to distinguish the erotic from the pornographic by arguing that the erotic tends "to evoke what we think to be the appropriate response of sexual interest which is more sensuous and voluptuous than lewd or prurient," while the pornographic tends to arouse a sexual response which she characterizes as lewd and licentious rather than sensuous (1984, 149). From Kittay's perspective, pornography is an illegitimate expression of sexuality because it is immoral to use another person for one's own pleasure ("use" can be real or fictive and "person" can mean either an individual or an image of an individual) (159).

Similarly, Susan Wendell claims that pornography "is intrinsically offensive to the dignity of women" (1983, 56) and that men who internalize the conviction of the equality between women and men "must recognize that the pleasurable responses they get from pornography are inappropriate to that conviction . . . " (55). According to Wendell, pornography depicts women as inferior, masochistic, and "primarily of value as instruments for the satisfaction of male lust" (54). Rosemarie Tong adds that women are offended, or should be offended, "by depictions of men treating women as pieces of meat ready to be branded or butchered on the altar of male sexual entertainment" (1982, 8).

It may be, however, that feminist norms for appropriate sexual expression fail to do justice to the genuine diversity among women in terms of sexual experiences and practices. One such practice is masturbation and the use of sexual fantasy which often accompanies it. This issue has raised discomforting questions for feminists about the appropriate use of sexual fantasy materials, particularly pornography, and has effectively placed personal confessions of masturbatory fantasies, dream-images and other reveries on political trial. Problems of how to achieve and maintain appropriate, rather than inappropriate, sexual feelings do not begin for women, or men, only at the threshold of a relationship with another person.

Robin Morgan has written about her personal struggle with sadomasochistic sexual fantasies. Although these fantasies stimulated her sexually, they disturbed her because they seemed to reinforce a sense of her inferiority to men. Morgan said she "refused to let myself fantasize any more," although "this precipitously reduced my capacity for orgasm . . . " (1982, 113-14). In a similar vein, Gregg Blachford has observed that some feminists reject the libertarian view of pornography that would allow men, and women, to use the sexually objectified images of pornography for their personal, and presumably masturbatory, pleasure. According to Blachford, these feminists—Susan Brownmiller is his primary example—say that "individuals are not simply 'doing their own thing' when masturbating to sexist images of women" but are "objectifying and therefore oppressing all women" (1978/1979, 23).

An agenda for politically correct sex, whether supplied by a feminist ideology or by religious authorities, threatens to police the intrapsychic arena of dreams and to create norms for autoerotic as well as interpersonal sexuality. On this proposed model of egalitarian sexuality, any erotic mental imagery conjured by one's imagination must, it seems, represent the sexual others only as summoned and respected guests who may not be disrobed, sexually enjoyed, or otherwise fantasized about against their wishes. But is this how the imagination constructs its images?

Power

Power has been a particularly difficult theme in American feminist discussions of pornography and female sexuality. Feminists opposed to pornography have argued that it is really about power and not about sex at all. In this view, power is seen as harmful to a vision of appropriate sexuality where relations of equality should rule. Irene Diamond, in the feminist journal *Signs*, spoke for many antipornography feminists when she called the "what" of pornography "not sex but power and violence" (1980, 689). Writing about pornography in a 1981 issue of the film studies journal *Jump Cut*, Valerie Miner said that "pornography is more about the exercise of power than about the expression of sex" (48).

Sally Wagner, writing against lesbian sadomasochism, offered one of the less conflicted feminist denunciations of power as an issue in representations of sexuality, such as pornography, and in sexual activity between persons. For Wagner, power over another is the "main obstacle" to sexual freedom, and sexual freedom will be possible "only when we break the connection between sex and power, when there is no power component in sexual interactions" (1982, 31,30). Wagner expressed a desire for a "transformed world in which power does not exist in human relationships . . . " (39). Lorna Weir and Leo Casey have observed that debates about power and sexuality are not limited to issues of sadomasochism but touch on problems of unequal relations in romantic roles as well (1984, 140). Feminist arguments of this type suggest that women's sexuality is unlike men's inherently "violent" sexuality and that women are interested only in what Linda Williams termed "a pure and natural pleasure uncontaminated by power" (1989, 20).

Other feminists have been less able to excise from the sexual script the part that power has played. Judy Butler noted that power and sex are inextricably intertwined and that "there is no immediate access to power-free sexuality," given the current historical and political situation. For Butler, however, power need not be taken on the terms it has been offered but may be "reshaped and deepened" to meet women's needs (1982, 173). Similarly, Amber Hollibaugh, writing with Cherrie Moraga, recognized that power is a legitimate part of sexuality if also a staple of a heterosexual construction of sexuality: "I don't want to live outside of power in my sexuality, but I don't want to be trapped into a heterosexist concept of power either" (1981, 59). In "Feminism and Sexuality in the 1980s," B. Ruby Rich critiqued what she saw as a popular "utopian ideal of equal power relations" and offered feminists a view of human sexuality inextricably tied to the infant's earliest relations to its parents, which meant that "all sexual relations seem to concern some kind of power dis-equilibrium, some kernel of psychic domination or surrender . . . " (1986, 547).

Feminists have defended power in sexual expression, including pornography, in a number of ways. Writing in the special "Sex Issue" of *Heresies*, Sandra Whisler remarked that her decision to masturbate, while remaining celibate in sexual relations with others, enabled her to realize that she had given men the power to make her feel satisfied and that this power "in fact belongs to me, is a part of my own personal power" (1981, 26). And for Ann Ferguson, even sexual representation that features images of dominance and submission may "empower" some women to enjoy sex more fully and thereby help develop "self-affirmation" (1984, 110).

Other defenses have been even more forceful. In her 1982 "Towards a Feminist Erotica," Kathy Myers argued that power does not function only to hold down or repress women's sense of pleasure and sexuality. Power can be seen as a "positive force" which actually produces forms of pleasure and sexuality and "provides the groundwork for a feminist erotica" (14). For Lisa Orlando, pornography is not only about the victimization of women; it also offers portrayals of women "taking and demanding pleasure, aggressive and powerful in a way rarely seen in our culture" (1982, 16).

A 1981 article, "Talking Sex: A Conversation on Sexuality and Feminism," brought together well-known feminists Deirdre English, Amber Hollibaugh, and Gayle Rubin. Hollibaugh highlighted the issue of power in sexual relationships by remarking that lesbian sex has been offered as the power-free alternative to heterosexual relationships but that "when you acknowledge power between women—that you would like to be dominated or dominate another woman in a sexual exchange, that you lust after her . . . ," one is told that a heterosexual model for sexual expression has contaminated one's lesbian sexual expression (44). As Hollibaugh had written elsewhere, "doing it side by side doesn't guarantee that sex is free of any fantasy of power . . . " (1984, 408).

A particularly striking example of the radically divergent ways feminists have understood the presence of power in sexual expression has been the case of the female stripper's work. In *Pornography and Silence: Culture's Revenge Against Nature*, Susan Griffin asserted that "to be made an object is in itself a humiliation" (1981, 47) and offered the striptease as a case in point. To Griffin, male voyeurs turn the innocent act of a woman removing her clothes into a sadistic act and a degradation. The male, "hidden in the darkness of a theater," "owns and masters" the woman. "He is in the position of power" (48).

Other writers offer a very different perspective on the location of power in the work of a stripper. As Marcia Pally has observed, "stripping is supposed to be the bottom of the sexist barrel, and women aren't supposed to overpower the men who watch them. But they do" (1985, 71). For feminist film maker Lizzie Borden, interviewed by Scott MacDonald, "in stripping and to an extent in pornography, and in prostitution, women often feel an enormous sense of power" (1989, 330). Writing about her own experience as a stripper, Seph Weene created an impression very different from Griffin's about how power and sexuality mix. Weene saw herself not as the passive and vulnerable victim of a sadistic male but as one who was powerful and in complete control of the sexual exchange between herself as a performer and the men in the audience: "The thrill I got from stripping was power." For Weene, unlike the hypothetical woman in Griffin's book, the stripper was the "dynamic force" and the audience was a "passive" presence. Weene wrote, "[W]hen a stripper's show is going well, the air is thick, charged with sexuality, and she is in total control" (1981, 36).

Sally Wagner's vision of "a transformed world in which power does not exist in human relationships" (1982, 39) or a feminist perspective that, in Alice Echols' words, "assume[s] that power simply withers away in egalitarian relationships" (1984, 66) may not promise women as much sexual satisfaction as could an exploration of the role of power in pleasure, which Linda Williams sees as something women have been taught to ignore in themselves (1989, 217). Perhaps power is always a part of sexual pleasure. As Williams observed, though one need not view power as "fixed," women may have to gain "a new consciousness about the unavoidable role of power in sex, gender, and sexual representations . . . " (228). Esther Newton and Shirley Walton add, "[W]e suspect that when we know more, we will find that power exchange is a central part of sexuality. If so, women will not be freed by flattening sexual experience in the name of equality" (1984, 250).

Sexual Fantasy

For numbers of feminists, the discussion of pornography invariably turns on the controversial issue of the relation of fantasy to acts or behavior. Writing about lesbian sadomasochism, Pat Califia suggested that fantasy was the key to understanding this consensual sexual practice whose scenes could be played out "using the personae of guard and prisoner, cop and suspect, Nazi and Jew . . . priest and penitent, teacher and student, whore and client, etc." For Califia, "it is not a felony to fantasize committing an illegal act," and the attempt to do away with sadomasochistic pornography amounted to "the equivalent of making fantasy a criminal act" (1981, 31-34). However, feminists convinced that there is a causal link between fantasy and behavior have been unwilling to allow any purgative or otherwise erotically satisfying role to works of pornography or to consensual sexual acts whose participants must assume roles of domination and submission. Although Susan Sontag, in her 1969 "The Pornographic Imagination," had observed that "everyone has felt (at least in fantasy) the erotic glamour of physical cruelty and an erotic lure in things that are vile and repulsive" (57), for many feminists the conflation of pornography and violence has meant that admitting to pornographic fantasies must be taken as admitting to aggression as well.

On this view, to use pornography or to entertain any "pornographic" mental images of women becomes evidence of men's hatred of women. But, as Carole Vance and Ann Snitow remarked, the antipornography movement, with its emphasis on violence, narrowed the meaning of pornography so that the "visual representation or objectification" of women in pornography became "first in a metaphorical sense and finally in a literal sense, violent" (1984, 129). Dorchen Leidholdt, for example, noting that it "has long exerted a powerful if unrecognized influence over sexual fantasies," indicted pornography for using women as things and creating fantasies out of the "victimization" of real women (1984, 38). Other feminists have been unwilling to equate fantasy with victimizing acts or behavior. Although clear about her own discomfort with masturbating to sexual fantasies she felt were sadomasochistic, Robin Morgan distinguished between fantasy and "real-life" acts of this type of sexual expression: "I know that I myself (and most of the women with whom I share the penchant for such fantasies) would never seek their reality" (1982, 115).

One may wish to question whether masturbation accompanied by mental imagery ever escapes the criticism that it treats as things the images of the real women, and men, it uses. That such sexual objectification fails to amount to violence against live human subjects has found little support among antipornography feminists, despite remarks of other feminists such as film critic Claire Pajakowska, who noted that "if pornographic images (especially in film) work within the same register as fantasy—predominantly the register of the Imaginary—then pornography is more likely to cause masturbation than rape" (1980, 14).

A common feminist question has been "To what extent do patriarchal relations determine our sexual fantasies and practices?" (Valverde 1989, 237). And at least one feminist has proposed that "fantasy, as an aspect of sexuality, may be a phallocentric 'need' from which we are not yet free" (Penelope 1980, 103). Likewise, Susanne Kappeler has argued that fantasy—"the unadulterated pleasure of the subject"—is part of the fundamental solipsism of the male culture which validates the viewing male subject who prefers looking at images of women to "the (troublesome) interaction with another subject," while objectifying the woman and depriving her of her own subjectivity (1986, 59-61). If men have constructed subjectivity in a way that makes women into objects, then visual pleasure—including the mental imagery or fantasy which may accompany sexual behavior—becomes politically suspect. Men's masturbatory images of women may be untrue to the reality of women, victimizing them by producing what feminist film critic Laura Mulvey termed "an illusion cut to the measure of desire" (1985, 314).

Whether men's eroticized images of women are cinematic or intrapsychic, the pleasure they provide is suspect if they are pornographic in character. According to Deirdre English, however, writing in "The Politics of Porn: Can Feminists Walk the Line?," feminist attempts to define the precise grounds on which to indict pornography and salvage erotica have led to arguably humorous political platforms such as "the Movement Against Your Right to Have Fantasies About Me" and "the Movement Against Your Right to Impose Your Fantasies on Me" (1980, 23, 43.) Although Nancy Friday's popular collections of women's sexual fantasies confirmed a wide range of imaginal, and often quite graphic and genital, interests among the women who responded to her surveys—and led one of her male critics to accuse her of reducing women to men's sexual level—feminists have declared that collections of "masochistic" fantasies, though understandable given their place in a patriarchal world, are nothing that women should be proud of.

Recording her own struggle with sexual feelings about cruel men as well as her genuinely erotic feelings for women, Andrea Dworkin said that "women experience so much sadomasochism that it becomes the only way we can come to sexuality" (1978, 57). Sally Wagner, too, acknowledged that "women are certainly going to have sexual fantasies that involve dominance and submission because this is how we have learned to experience our sexuality," but went on to ask, "[W]hat do we choose to do about these fantasies?" (1982, 39). At one stage of her struggle with sadomasochistic fantasies, the choice of Robin Morgan was to refuse to let herself fantasize, though this significantly reduced her capacity for orgasm (1982, 113-14).

One feminist response to the question of what pleasures, including fantasy, are possible for women under a patriarchal order has been to refuse the terms of engagement entirely. And yet, the agenda of refusing all politically incorrect inducements to sexual expression, including the lure of one's own patriarchally constructed and contaminated sexual fantasies—in short, refusing to play the "male" sexual game—has not won favor with all feminists. For example, Alice Echols remarked that to require a feminist sexuality to eliminate power was to encourage feminists "to renounce our sexuality as it is now," and to alienate women from psychological and social sources of sexual power (1984, 58). It may indeed be the case, as Jessica Benjamin has pointed out, that a man as well as a woman can be "the slave of love"; and given the culture we live in, the fantasy of erotic domination, "which mingles love, control, and submission," is part of normal adult love relationships (1980, 144).

Exploring the Alternatives

An alternative to a utopian feminist agenda that would argue celibacy or separatism has been the suggestion that women have something to gain by exploring their own sexuality and erotic taboos as they exist. For example, Paula Webster asked about the numbers of women "who almost defiantly say they have *no* fantasies, or no *need* to act them out." For Webster concern with sexual taboo has stopped even women's imaginings. "How many times have we resisted knowing what it is that might give us erotic pleasure?" (1984, 388).

Joanna Russ observed that knowledge of women's "real sexual histories" is not synonymous with women's political opinions, and she acknowledged that to feel and express these histories "demands an honesty that will, at times, produce intense shame and (I would expect) feelings of defeat and self-condemnation." For Russ, what is required of feminists is "the gritty reality of what we really feel, what we really want"—regardless of how disgusting, wrong, or anti-feminist it might seem (1987, 39-40).

Carole Vance and Ann Barr Snitow cautioned feminists not to allow "new prescriptions" for feminist sexuality to destroy an atmosphere of candor regarding the actual range of sexual behavior and fantasy that characterizes women's sexual experience (1984, 134). According to Vance and Snitow, women need to create "a climate for the safe telling and hearing of our particular sexual histories" (135). They note that, ironically, the strong antipornography focus on the dominant patriarchal order has resulted in two sexual silences: "silence about what women actually do and silence about what images women find arousing" (132). In the foreword to her 1989 study of hard-core pornography, Linda Williams wrote about the difficulty facing a feminist who would admit to *any* sexual interest in pornography: "I know that the slightest admission that not every image of every film was absolutely disgusting to me may render my insights worthless to many women . . . " (xi).

In a special issue of *The Journal of Sex Research* devoted to feminist perspectives on sexuality, Lisa Duggan criticized historical discussions of sex for their alleged inattention to what really transpires between individuals in sexual behavior. Duggan wrote: "Oddly, as the discussion of 'sexuality' has exploded in intellectual circles, the specification of acts—what people actually do when they 'have sex' and how these acts have changed over time—has seldom been attempted" (1990, 109).

It may be that human sexual practice does not readily conform to rational directives or theoretical requirements. According to Muriel Dimen, sexuality, because of its irrationality, is not a domain where it makes sense "to pull behavior into line with ideology" (1984, 144). Bodies seem to have minds of their own. But this *apologia* for sexual unruliness has come under fire from those who question the existence of an innate sexual impulse.

Until relatively recently, it has been possible to single out the physical body as a primary place where irrational sexual desires defeat political and religious commitments and to pose sexual desire as the fixed and recalcitrant opponent of any ideology. Recent thinking, much of it feminist in origin, has challenged this view. If bodies are always imaginal as well as biological, and if sexual desire, once taken for a visceral certitude, is socially constructed, that is, shaped by historical and geopolitical circumstance, then human sexual expression may be more cannily ideological than straightforwardly physiological in the "truth" it reveals about human nature.

Feminists have argued that it is no longer really defensible for a woman or a man to assert the validity of personal sexual interests by appealing to bodily evidence—vaginal secretions or erections—as testimony to a "natural" or unconstituted sexual desire. For example, Catharine MacKinnon has argued that although in our culture "body is widely regarded as access to unmediated truth," a woman's physiological arousal to pornography—vaginal secretions—is a Pavlovian conditioned response to social cues about sexuality rather than objective proof of her genuine sexual interest (1989, 338-39). And Gayle Rubin, from a feminist position virtually opposite that of MacKinnon, has written that "we never encounter the body unmediated by the meanings that cultures give to it" (1984, 276-77).

In "Pleasure and Danger: Toward a Politics of Sexuality," Carole Vance doubtless spoke for numbers of women who take seriously the need to understand sexuality in a non-biological way but find that the particularities of individual women, especially in their sexual practices, must not be dismissed as irrelevant or improper. Vance asked, "Do we distrust our passion, thinking it perhaps not our own, but the construction of patriarchal culture?" (1984, 6). "What is the nature of the relationship between the arbitrariness of social construction and the immediacy of our bodily sensations and functions?" (9). Can women who view their sexuality as socially constructed still comfortably claim what Dorothy Dinnerstein called "the brute sense of bodily prerogative, of having a right to one's bodily feelings" (1976, 73)?

Despite its effect of requiring women "to renounce our sexuality as it is now" (Echols 1984, 58), some feminists have deemed it politically appropriate to deny that any genuine pleasure is possible for women under patriarchy. But, as Carole Vance suggested, to let patriarchy dictate the terms of engagement for women is perhaps to reinforce the role of women as victims and to deny that they can be sexual actors (1984, 6). While it may be politically compelling for women to come out against the evils of patriarchy, it is surely worth asking whether, in contrast to a "phallic" sexuality, a female sexuality can be constructed that would be credible. And numbers of feminists have agreed with Linda Williams that it is erroneous to suggest that a female sexuality free of patriarchal contaminations "would express no violence, would have no relations of power, and would produce no transgressive sexual fantasies" (1989, 20).

Perhaps pornography exists because it is about transgressive sexual fantasies and cannot be made into politically correct erotica. It may also be the case that fantasies about normal sexual behavior do not speak to many individuals' situations. Julia Lesage asked, "What is degrading? If we are honest about what we, our friends, our lovers, children get off on, what do we find?" (1981, 46). In a straightforward testimonial to the emotional complexities of sexual expression, Lesage offered a context for understanding her own question about what it might mean for men to have violent and transgressive fantasies about women: sex "always expresses some aspect of interpersonal relations"—including, in addition to love, "hostility, anger, dependency, power, submission . . ." (47).

A common strategy for feminists opposed to pornography has been to see in its images only men's hatred of women. The work of Deirdre English, and others like her, however, represents an equally well-articulated feminist appraisal of pornography but one that has focused instead on pornography's role as a "vehicle of rebellion against sexual and moral norms." English stated that "pornography depends on shock value. It lives to violate taboos" (1980, 48). Writing about women and pornography, Jean Callahan asked whether the appeal of pornography "is that it is not safe, that it is taboo—taboo because it shows the extremes of desire, the extremes of pleasure and pain, and, most important, power stretched to its limits" (1982, 63). And stripper Seph Weene acknowledged that "both the conventional, male-dominated outlook and feminist doctrine defined what I did as bad. I was having forbidden fun" (1981, 37).

Pornography and a Feminist Agenda for Sexuality

Is it possible for feminists, or anyone else, to debate the merits and the meaning of pornography without at the same time offering a vision of what sexual satisfaction should look like? The question of pornography inevitably raises the issue of the philosophy of sexuality one is willing to espouse. Though not all objections to pornography have been expressed in terms which suggest there is an inherent way that human sexuality is meant to be practiced, many critics of pornography, feminist or otherwise, have agreed with Robin Morgan that "pornography is sexist propaganda" and that it transforms "that most intimate, vulnerable, and tender of physical exchanges into one of conquest and humiliation . . . ." (1977, 168).

An alternative to Morgan's indictment of patriarchy as the root cause of pornography may lie in Lisa Orlando's suggestion that "a Rousseauean belief in benign *human* nature" undergirds at least part of the feminist antipornography platform, despite the common feminist preference for seeing sexuality as a social construction. "Anti-porn feminists want to believe that if the negative effects of patriarchal conditioning were removed (from men and bad girls—good girls are somehow closer to nature), we would all be equally 'moral' and 'erotic' (read feminine)" (1982, 18).

Is pornography, with its images of transgressive sexuality, an exclusively male disease, or does it present a particular truth about sexuality that applies to women as well as men? Writing about the pornographic fiction of Georges Bataille, and with specific reference to both Andrea Dworkin's relentless assault on the male pornographic sensibility and Susan Sontag's assessment of Bataille's work, Susan Rubin Suleiman may have posed the dilemma of pornography for feminists clearly: "What Sontag saw as the revelation of a troubling truth about human sexuality, Dworkin diagnoses as the particular truth of *male* desire, or the male imagination of sex, in our culture" (1986, 125).

What, then, might be the particular truth of female desire? At the close of her 1982 *Screen* article, "The Body As Evidence: A Critical Review of the Pornography Problematic," Lesley Stern wrote, "[I]t may well turn out that female fantasy is not singular and certainly contradictory, that the intertwinings of sex and death and violence are not uniquely male properties" (n.pag.). In the introduction to *Powers of Desire*, editors Ann Snitow, Christine Stansell, and Sharon Thompson asked whether it was possible in the service of a feminist sexual politics to exercise "rational control" over fantasy and whether there should be a sexual ethics that extends to fantasy. Was all objectification of others necessarily dehumanizing and alienated? Or "is it inevitable that we sometimes see our lovers as objects, as things we wish to shape to our passion and will" (1983, 40)?

In a 1984 *Socialist Review* essay dealing with the relation of pornography to the feminist imagination, Kate Ellis characterized "the pornographic mind" in terms very close to the ones Snitow, Stansell, and Thompson supplied in asking about the inevitabilities of caring sexual expression between lovers. Ellis inquired about women's potential for a pornographic mind, which she described as "one that images the object of desire and tries to possess, control, and deprive him/her of any vestige of a will" (112). She concluded that "what is irrational in us" is worth exploring, "not in order to let exploitation loose in the world but in order to deepen mutuality" (122).

What is particularly provocative is the suggestion, arrived at by combining the remarks of Ellis with those of Snitow, Stansell, and Thompson, that the irrational and transgressive expressions represented by pornography may not be intrusions ill-suited to the intimacies of sexual expression between lovers but rather part and parcel of what sexual desire entails, and that mutuality may be furthered not by attempting to purge the psyche of its politically inappropriate fantasies but by letting those psychic images speak to us.

Finally, is not the objectifying desire to shape others to our passion and will—the "pornographic" wish to deprive another of any vestige of a will—not what many have understood as sexual lust (or concupiscence, in Christian terms)? According to some feminists, lust is one form of sexual desire that has been problematic in feminist discussions of sexuality. Amber Hollibaugh, for example, claimed that lust is problematic for lesbian feminists because lust acknowledges the presence of power between women—"that you would like to be dominated or dominate another woman in a sexual exchange" (English, Hollibaugh, Rubin 1981, 44). And Ellen Willis observed that some feminists are wary of any egalitarian model of sexuality that offers "unfettered male lust" as a model for both sexes. "It's safer if female sexuality is different—maybe we don't want to be unfettered" (1981, 36).

Christians even more than feminists have been ideologically identified with issues involving sexual lust or inordinate sexual desire. Christians too have been in the forefront of the antipornography movement, defending appropriate sexual expression from its pornographic defilements. What, then, is one to make of Susan Griffin's contention that "every theme, every attitude, every shade of pornographic feeling has its origin in the church" (1981, 16)?

Chapter 4

Christian Perspectives on Sex and Pornography

An examination of the work of feminists with an avowed interest in religion or spirituality reveals a vision of sexuality in which equality is foundational. However, a mandate for equality in matters of sexual expression encounters resistance in the form of the decidedly selfish quest of the physical body for pleasure and the vagaries of sexual excitement that constitute that quest. Both sexual excitement and the alleged selfishness of the sex drive have been problems for Christian theological reflection. Pornography has presented Christians across a spectrum of confessional identities not only with a decidedly strong challenge to their interpretation of what constitutes the proper expression of human sexuality but also, more recently, with graphic examples of what many see as the continuing mistreatment of women in our culture. The cultural problem of pornography for both contemporary Christians and feminists has been decisively shaped by traditional Christian constructions of the sexual imagination. Moreover, significant feminist objections to pornography are isomorphic with Christian ones in the emphasis both place on the transgressive possibilities of sexual fantasy. This common emphasis raises the possibility that certain feminist arguments are formally, if unwittingly, Christian, even while being apparently against Christian patriarchalism.

Feminism and Sexual Equality

Recent feminist scholarship has questioned the intuitive assumption that pornography is, or should be, repugnant to Christian women and men because it is about unbridled, and therefore illicit, sexual excitement. In "Pornography: An Agenda for the Churches," which appeared in *The Christian Century*, Mary Pellauer challenged Christian churches to be concerned about pornography because it is "violent or actively degrading to women" rather than because it is sexual (1987, 653). Although she observed that Christian tradition has not been particularly helpful when it comes to affirming any sexual expression apart from procreation (653), she stated her belief that "no one who celebrates healthy sexuality among the many goods of God's creation can affirm pornography" (655). In a 1989 essay, "Pornography and the Religious Imagination," Mary Jo Weaver argued that the connection between Christianity and pornography "does not rest with Christian teachings about sex but with traditional Christian teaching about women as inherently inferior" (69-70). For Weaver pornography is "an intensification of the gender differences in traditional Christianity," a "further distortion of the already distorted social roles" embodied in the Christian religious vision (77). Mary Ellen Ross, writing in *The Christian Century* in 1990, appealed to Christians and feminists to respond concretely to the destructive influence of pornography and asserted that pornographers share with many Christian thinkers "contempt for human physicality and for women" (246). According to Ross, "the critical feature of all pornography is not that it deals with sexual themes, but that it eroticizes violence, humiliation, degradation and other explicit forms of abuse" (244).

Feminist objections to pornography which target its role in patriarchal distortions of gender equality, its refusal to see that "both sexes were made in the image of God" (Ross 1990, 246), rather than its sexual themes raises the implicit question of what egalitarian, nonpatriarchal sexual representation and sexual behavior—good sex—should be. For one thing, according to feminists, good sex must be mutual and unitive and not combative or hostile.

Writing in *Women's Consciousness, Women's Conscience: A Reader in Feminist Ethics*, Catherine Keller disputed Simone de Beauvoir's Hegelian claim in *The Second Sex* that "we find in consciousness itself a fundamental hostility toward every other consciousness" (1971, xvii). For Keller, some "fundamental hostility" may indeed characterize "the psychological metaphysic of male sovereignty," but "what price are we to pay as women if we 'authentically assume' *this* subjective attitude?" Though not writing specifically about pornography or sexuality, Keller's assertion that a fundamental hostility may not "disclose the essence of any human subject whatsoever" (1985, 255) suggests that in a feminist vision of sexual practice, self and other are not necessarily alienated by a foundational or constitutional antagonism, trapped by a patriarchal psychological assessment of subjectivity whose limiting conditions, particularly with respect to hostility, apply to women as well as men.

Above all, good sex must embody mutuality. In *Touching Our Strength: The Erotic as Power and the Love of God*, feminist theologian Carter Heyward has written that "our sexualities are our embodied yearning to express a relational mutuality" and that individuals must "act sexually only in mutual relationships, in which the erotic moves between us to evoke that which is most fully human in each of us" (1989, 33, 129). For Heyward, pornography abuses the agapeic quality of eros (95, 177). Good sex is based on friendship (33) and involves lovers who are "committed gently, patiently, and playfully to calling one another into being and touching one another into life" (134-35). Good sex is characterized by a profound sense of tenderness (135).

Theologian Beverly Wildung Harrison has suggested that in a new Christian paradigm for sexuality, one that takes account of the rising consciousness of women (1984, 146), sexuality comes to mean "our embodied sensuous capacity for relationship" (154). In this new, feminist, paradigm, "mutuality, or genuine reciprocity, is utterly foundational" (149). And for Heyward, "even in moments of erotic ecstacy" or sexual orgasm, in "the coming together of self and other," it is "friendship" that "brings us into this excitement . . . " (1989, 33).

The articulation of a feminist consciousness in which mutuality, friendship, or reciprocity is the foundation for healthy relationships finds support in a 1987 article by Mary Ellen Ross. According to Ross, the autonomous, Freudian psychological man who must confront the limited possibilities of the human enterprise in the face of "the inevitability of hierarchical power relationships" (157) is no longer valid as an ethical model for women and men. Freud's view of the hierarchical social order as necessary and thus inevitable is challenged by feminists for whom "the possibility of the demise of hierarchy is the main hope and primary article of faith" (158). Toward this vision of a new earth Ross consecrates the work of feminist activists who have created "egalitarian" communities and of feminist writers and artists who "have produced images of equal relationships between women and men" (166).

In an essay in *Christianity, Patriarchy, and Abuse,* Harrison and Heyward have challenged the "pessimistic" assumption that eroticism must inevitably be experienced "as a choice between self- and other-enhancement," and have argued that the goal of feminist ethics and politics should be to "affirm the possibility that eros . . . can enhance mutuality" (1989, 164-165). In a patriarchal culture that does not understand the intrinsically "social" character of selfhood (164), self and other are pitted against one another in a "dualistic praxis" where few are able to find their way to "full eroticization in mutuality." For Harrison and Heyward, feminists must repudiate "the association of eroticism with the split between self and other that is endemic to the patriarchal view of reality." The loss of patriarchal tension between self and other, however, "is experienced unavoidably as the diminishment or elimination of erotic power" and may help to explain why "so many people (feminists and others) find it hard to sustain high levels of sexual excitement in the context of friendship" (162).

That the call to politically correct sex may threaten to diminish some of the intensities associated with sexual arousal has been noted also by political scientist Donald Alexander Downs, in *The New Politics of Pornography* (1989). Downs observed that progressive critiques of sexuality and sexual practice "recoil from the animalistic or biological aspects of sexuality, seeking refuge in a political meaning designed to purify sexual relations in the name of equality" (184). As Murray S. Davis has argued in *Smut: Erotic Reality/Obscene Ideology,* a certain feminist concern to abolish sex that is not democratic and egalitarian actually is "inspired by the spirit of an old-fashioned fundamentalist religion." According to Davis, "only the heirs to a puritanical ideology . . . would consider abolishing sex entirely to end whatever taint of inequality there may be in it" (1983, 172).

Numbers of religious feminists seem to be suggesting a new vision of sexuality where egalitarianism in sexual pleasure somehow can surpass the pleasure available under patriarchal constructions of eroticism where self and other are separated and a personal quest for pleasure may threaten the symmetrical structure of egalitarian relationships. Something about the pleasures of sexual excitement, at least under the conditions of patriarchy, often make them seem incompatible with friendship.

Sexual Excitement and Selfishness

Sexual excitement has not been an easy topic for numbers of theological writers. Christian ethicist James B. Nelson has written that even those Christians who affirm the goodness and holiness of sex "leave the subject of pleasure largely unexplored and unaffirmed." To affirm sexual pleasure too boldly may seem to "invite self-indulgence and destroy true spirituality and communion" (1983, 36-37). Harrison and Heyward observed that many religious feminists have failed to explore specific questions of eros and sex, and they offer their own work as an attempt to deal with "women's eroticism and genital pleasure" (1989, 149).

Intense sexual pleasure has been an issue of great substance for Christian thinkers in various historical periods. From very early on, sexual excitement has been seen as a drain on the will seeking to gain freedom from "lusts and desires and the other passions." According to early Christian theologian Clement of Alexandria, the Christian ideal of continence was not to experience desire at all. Even desire "quiescent so far as bodily action is concerned" meant that the will was neither chaste nor controlled. "For we are children not of desire but of will" (1954, ch. 7, sect. 57-58).

In *The City of God* Augustine had observed that the pleasure which resulted from "the lustful excitement of the organs of generation" was "the greatest of all bodily pleasures." "So possessing indeed is this pleasure, that at the moment of time in which it is consummated, all mental activity is suspended" (1950, bk. 14, sect. 16). According to Augustine, the "violent acting of lust" and "wild heat of passion" disturb the calmness of mind which is required if the sexual act is not to corrupt the integrity of the body (bk. 14, sect. 26).

Medieval historian James Brundage has argued that Christian preoccupation with the missionary position for human sexual intercourse reflected a suspicion on the part of theologians and canonists that "pleasure and posture might be related" (1984, 82) and that variations in sexual practice were being pursued in order to intensify physical pleasure. According to Brundage, one canonist apparently held "that if the partners employed novel positions in order to heighten their enjoyment, they sinned mortally" (86).

Contemporary Christian reflection continues the traditional suspicion that intense sexual pleasure, with its clogging of consciousness, is selfish or self-centered, thus arguably limiting one's capacity for mutuality in love making. In *Sexual Happiness in Marriage*, conservative Christian sociologist Herbert Miles observed that "when the husband and wife are in their orgasms they are in a state of semi-consciousness and can do little or nothing by way of helping the other, or being aware of what the other is doing or experiencing" (1982, 108). Writing in *Sex: Thoughts for Contemporary Christians*, Sidney Cornelia Callahan noted that "pleasurable violence" and "possessiveness" characterize the genital drive—hardly a prescription for treating another's sexual needs as equal to one's own in a moment of intense physiological pleasure (1972, 153). In *Christianity and Eros*, Philip Sherrard exemplified the Christian concern that inordinate sexual desire or excitement is selfish. Leaning on Augustine for support, Sherrard wrote that lust is "essentially a desire for self-satisfaction." "In lust, it is the self which is the centre of attraction, and the object which stimulates it is simply an object and nothing more" (1976, 45).

It may not be surprising, then, that Christian injunctions against seeking one's own pleasure in sex have been seen by sex therapists, including Christian therapists, as contributing to a lack of sexual happiness among many married couples. In *Sexual Problems in Marriage*, a book heavily influenced by the work of Masters and Johnson, F. Philip Rice observed that some wives are too worried about whether or not they are pleasing their husbands and consequently forego their own sexual arousal. Christian counselor Rice recommended that the woman seeking (but not finding) sexual pleasure concentrate on her own feelings, "be selfish," and, for a time, not worry about how her husband is feeling (1978, 210). The husband with trouble achieving or maintaining an erection was advised "to be 'selfish,' to let his wife pleasure him, and not to be concerned with her reactions or thoughts for the time being" (171). Rice's seemingly unChristian recommendation to "be selfish" in the quest for sexual pleasure hints at another, equally provocative aspect of a vision of human sexuality owing much to the work of Masters and Johnson: masturbation. In its emphasis on the physiology of sex, *Human Sexual Response* (1966) had provocatively focused the traditional Christian dilemma of the body's selfish quest for pleasure when it declared unequivocally that, at least for women, masturbation produced a more intense orgasm than sexual intercourse (133). The testimony of the (female) body that the orgasm produced by coitus is not as intense as the one produced by masturbation raises for numbers of Christians a particular dilemma regarding sexual excitement: the most intense sexual pleasures—specifically masturbation, but perhaps oral sex as well—may be illicit or morally forbidden.

The Christian discomfort with the topic of sexual pleasure, noted by liberal theologian James Nelson (above), is evident across a wide spectrum of Christian theological belief. This discomfort is particularly clear in Roman Catholicism.

In *Christian Design for Sex*, Joseph Buckley affirmed that masturbation, "the seeking of the willful enjoyment of carnal pleasure," was always a mortal sin, but conceded that "the natural significance of a loving giving-away of oneself is still inherent in the act." However, "since there is no one there to receive this giving, it becomes a 'throwing away' of oneself" (1953, 43). Prodigality in the taking of one's sexual pleasures is forbidden. Sexual pleasure must be mutual, unitive, or it must not be at all.

The essential aim of conjugal intimacy—the sexual pleasure ordained by God—must always be toward the primary end of marriage, which is procreation. According to Catholic moral theologians John C. Ford and Gerald Kelly, the purpose of marital intimacy "is frustrated by any conduct which involves the unjustifiable risking of orgasm apart from intercourse," and any "deliberate consent to orgasm outside intercourse," including masturbation, amounts to "sinful hedonism" (1963, 196-197).

In 1975 the Magisterium, or teaching body, of the Roman Catholic Church reaffirmed traditional Catholic doctrine regarding masturbation: it is a practice "linked with a loss of the sense of God," "an intrinsically and seriously disordered act" which contradicts the "finality" of conjugal relations (in Kosnik 1977, 306).

Catholic moral theologians attempting to affirm the pleasures of human sexuality without contradicting the teaching of the Church regarding the subordinate ends of pleasure in the marital economy have had to do battle with a tradition that has denigrated sexual passion—often for its selfishness. In 1963 Cardinal Leon Suenens, former primate of Belgium, wrote: "love is never the combined selfishness of two people." According to Suenens, "in itself, the sexual instinct is self-centered, looks out for its own interests and rather tends to subjugate other people to its own ends, without respect for their dignity and independence as persons" (47).

Catholic theologian John C. Dwyer, wishing to counter the characterization of human sexuality as a ruthless instinct when not tempered by love, stated that "it should never be suggested that intense sexual pleasure is for some reason suspect" (1987, 58). For Dwyer, it is not the intensity of sexual pleasure but the failure to add agape to sensuality that marks the destructive aspect of eroticism. Those individuals who make intense pleasure itself the goal of sexual activity, who are "totally indifferent to the personal existence of the one with whom they are engaged in sexuality activity," have failed to appreciate sexuality as God intended it (59). It seems that Dwyer wants both to affirm the intensities of sexual pleasure and to guarantee that in the moments of pleasure there is no mental occlusion of, or indifference to, the needs of the other—in a vision of human sexual possibility that appears to deny the Augustinian contention that intense pleasure suspends the rationality presumably required for mindfulness of others' needs. Furthermore, in Dwyer's Catholic understanding of the unitive, other-directed function of human sexuality, masturbation is an "infantile fixation" (56). In Dwyer's attempt to validate the intensities of sexual pleasure, the particular sexual intensity of the masturbatory orgasm—this unrepentant physiological witness to the self-reflexive possibilities of the sexual body—is a forbidden pleasure.

One strategy that has enabled Christian thinkers to affirm the intensities of sexual pleasure while maintaining the ideologically correct posture that another's needs should be at least as important as one's own has been the organizing belief that, when simultaneously achieved, the orgasmic climax cancels the inherent self-centeredness of the sexual act and prevents the depersonalization of the partner. In *Love and Control: The Contemporary Problem*, Cardinal Suenens wrote that in the conjugal union "the resulting, natural, physical pleasure is not, primarily, a satisfaction that each partner achieves for himself but, psychologically, it is a joy which each first gives to the other before experiencing it fully himself." In the act of love one must put aside "natural selfishness." "To be fully experienced physically, this joy needs as much simultaneity as possible" (1963, 68).

Catholic theologian Marc Oraison noted that masturbation leaves a mark of selfishness on the individual who then "will remain deeply concerned with self-gratification whenever he exercises his sex activities, and in spite of himself he will experience marital intercourse as a form of self-abuse somehow made legitimate" (1958, 109). In sexual activity with his wife it is important that the man "synchronize the climax." The man who has been conditioned "by the habit of self-abuse" displays "a tendency toward precipitate action," a desire to go too fast, which reduces the woman "to the role of mere instrument" (111-112). A possible interpretation of Oraison's analysis would have at least male sexual urgency—what Augustine had called "the violent acting of lust"—seem a consequence of the willful indulgence in masturbation rather than a testimony to the body's own drive for unrestrained pleasure.

It is by no means only Roman Catholic theologians who seem to have a difficult time affirming sexual pleasures whose focus is the individual. In *Innocent Ecstasy*, Peter Gardella suggested that the prescription for "simultaneous orgasm" advanced by birth control advocate Margaret Sanger well before World War II and frequently observed in marriage manuals up to the present day offered a vision of conjugal union that "would be truly ecstatic, carrying each partner out of self and obliterating the distinctions between them" (1985, 134-135). Gardella saw in the emphasis on orgasm as a mystical event a shying away from the acknowledgement that as bodies we are "always separated from each other and from God by irreducible physical being" but that our separateness as bodies is what allows us to love (161).

Mutual orgasm—"synchronized climax"—may also be the orienting vision in liberal Christian theologian James B. Nelson's book *Embodiment*. While observing in apparent Augustinian fashion that "in pleasure of whatever sort, the will seems to recede and the ego surrenders some of its control over the body," Nelson goes on to say that in the "climax of sexual communion" the "body-self" may feel "taken out of itself into another" while also remaining "intensely itself" (1978, 87). In the "little death" of orgasm there occurs the "temporary sense of loss of self-conscious individuality, but with this comes the self's death in surrender to the other" (255). That is, in the pleasure of sexual orgasm one surrenders to another who is a self and not an object. Borrowing Dwyer's words, the sexual behavior must be the response of "*this woman* to *this man, this man* to *this woman*" (1987, 58-59). For

Nelson, it is "loveless" to engage in any sex act "obsessed solely by physical gratification" (128), and "an extreme focus upon genitality more frequently marks sexual alienation than it signifies sexual wholeness" (156).

The reluctance of many Christian thinkers to affirm sexual practices—such as masturbation and oral sex—which focus on a particular self rather than on genital intercourse between selves may reflect the belief that these practices create an emphasis on genitality untouched by agape and therefore diminish the obligation of sexual activity to be an expression of mutual love between two people.

The testimony to pleasure of the masturbatory orgasm has not been the only challenge to Christians concerned to constrain sexual arousal to the pleasures attending vaginal intercourse in a monogamous relationship of marriage. In 1966 Masters and Johnson had reported that, after masturbation, "the next highest level of erotic intensity has resulted from partner manipulation . . . and the lowest intensity . . . was achieved during coition" (133). Evidence that for some individuals pleasure from partner sex other than coition—oral sex, for example—may exceed that experienced in intercourse has been disconcerting.

Catholic moral theologians John C. Ford and Gerald Kelly had announced in 1963 that "all are agreed today that the wife is not entitled to orgasm outside a natural marriage act" (225). Sexual acts such as oral sex would be "grave sins against chastity" if they involved "a serious and unjustifiable risk of orgasm outside intercourse" (229).

Some conservative Protestant Christians have echoed this Catholic restriction on sex other than vaginal intercourse. Sociologist Herbert J. Miles, for example, claimed that oral sex "is not necessary for good sexual adjustment in marriage." He advised couples that oral sex "should never be considered superior to sexual intercourse" (1982, 157,160). Desire for oral sex reflected an exaggerated interest in "selfish gratification" (158). Husband and wife team Tim and Beverly LaHaye, in *The Act of Marriage*, said that oral sex was on the increase "thanks to amoral sex education, pornography, modern sex literature, and the moral breakdown of our times" (1976, 226). They expressed their doubt that oral sex was "as popular on a regular basis as most modern sexologists would have us think" (226) and reaffirmed their belief that, for a man, "intercourse is beyond comparison the most satisfying means of ejaculation" (28). Further, they expressed their confidence that "nothing will ever replace the traditional act of marriage as the favorite method of expressing sexual love between married partners" (226-227). More recently, Tim LaHaye has said that "if I were writing *The Act of Marriage* today, I would be more positive in speaking out against oral sex. Evidently I wasn't quite as clear as I thought I was being, but I am definitely opposed to it" (in Colman 1985, 118).

That sexual intercourse alone does not meet many women's desire for orgasm has been commonly recognized. For example, well-known sex therapist Helen Singer Kaplan, writing in 1974, said that "the failure to achieve orgasm on coitus by the woman who is otherwise fully responsive sexually is probably the most common sexual complaint currently encountered in sexual treatment centers" (377). According to journalist Deirdre English, "the rise in the number of female orgasms is probably directly related to what some sex researchers have called 'the real sexual revolution'—the astonishing rise of oral-genital sex among heterosexuals. Today, the majority of women enjoy what was once considered a perversion" (1980, 49).

And despite what the LaHayes claim about the satisfactions of genital intercourse for men, evidence suggests that some sexual acts—specifically, oral sex—may be more intensely pleasurable than vaginal intercourse. Sex therapist Avodah K. Offit observed that many men prefer fellatio to intercourse: "The various squeezing, scraping, and sucking actions that the mouth can perform far outnumber the possibilities for sensual variety inside a vagina." When one considers the possibilities for sensation of fellatio, she said, "the wonder sometimes seems to be that men like intercourse at all" (1981, 64-65).

Christian Objection to Pornography

Although pornographers might claim that their work is meant to represent images of exquisite sexual pleasure, tailored to the various and idiosyncratic sexual fantasies that make for human sexual arousal and excitement, Christians representing various theological perspectives and interests have condemned pornography without hesitation. Representations of sexual activities which are morally forbidden to numbers of Christians—sex outside marriage, sexual acts other than vaginal intercourse, sex that is lustful and excessively genital, sex which celebrates the physical to the apparent detriment of the emotional or which treats humans as sexual playthings—are a clear transgression of the Christian moral order under which personal sexual pleasure must never come at the apparent expense of another nor be the primary end or goal of human sexuality.

Writing in *Christianity Today* in 1958, Ralph A. Cannon and Glenn D. Everett called on church people concerned with preserving the sanctity of the Christian home to oppose *Playboy* and similar men's magazines which "de-personalized" women and showed them "as pliant machines which men utilize for brutish pleasure." The authors claimed that the libertine emphasis of these sex magazines amounted to "the most sustained and insidious attack on the moral standards of this nation ever witnessed in the history of our Republic" (6).

More recently, in "Pornography and Vice in the Media," Pope John Paul II indicted pornography for working against the "family character" of true human sexuality in its view of sexual activity as "a continuing frenzied search for personal gratification rather than . . . an expression of enduring love in marriage" (1989, 275). In their 1988 study, *Pornography: Far From The Song of Songs*, the Presbyterian Church (U.S.A.) task force noted that pornography's images of sexuality "violate God's images of human dignity and sexual pleasure based on mutual love and respect." Pornography also reflects and reinforces the view that "self-gratification is the highest good" (78).

An undated Southern Baptist pamphlet, "Issues & Answers: Pornography," states categorically that from a Christian perspective, "there is no defense for pornography." Pornography offers "a false and damaging view of sex," in which women are treated as things and the spiritual aspects of sex are missing. "Marital fidelity and chastity are undermined, and promiscuity, wife-trading, and sexual perversion are encouraged" (5).

In *Pornography: A Christian Critique*, John H. Court observed: "common sense and scientific evidence agree that exposure to erotica increases sexual arousal and the probability of sexual activity." For Court, "if one believes that intimate sexuality should be expressed privately within a relationship of commitment and love," then arousal to pornography becomes morally objectionable (1980, 43). In omitting the dimension of love from sexual expression "pornography represents a view of sexuality which is the very antithesis of a Christian and humane view" (68). Liberal Christian theologian James B. Nelson acknowledged that the issue of pornography required a balance between the right to publish and the right to read what one wanted, on the one hand, and "the rights of persons to be free from the intrusion of sexual materials deemed offensive and dehumanizing," on the other (1978, 262). He noted that the audience for pornography has typically been male and that pornography usually degrades women, showing them being used by men for male sexual pleasure (163).

Christians often base their objections to representations of sexual activity that arouse lascivious and prurient interests on words of Jesus from Matthew 5:28. There Jesus trumped the forefathers' understanding of adultery in the flesh by telling his hearers that "every one who looks at a woman lustfully has already committed adultery with her in his heart" (RSV). These words of Jesus, which Dwight Hervey Small saw as a warning against "looking that is lusting" (1974, 183), have functioned to modulate even the sexual desire one can express for a spouse.

The Dilemma of Sexual Fantasy

While Christian groups have been quick to condemn pornography as a particularly grievous distortion of human sexuality, a perversion of sex as God intended it, they have been less able to ask whether pornography may itself be an extrusion of the sexual imagination as Christianity has traditionally constructed it. Put simply, Christians have been more willing to deal with the presence of the pornographic outside themselves, in the world at large, than with the possibility that it resides as an imaginal possibility within even the most devout of believers. Susan Griffin suggested that pornography could be seen "as if it were a modern building, built on the site of the old cathedrals, sharing the same foundation." For her the old structure and the new are similar: "all the old shapes of religious asceticism are echoed in obscenity" (1981, 16).

In *The Ascetic Imperative in Culture and Criticism*, Geoffrey Galt Harpham has suggested that there is "an ascetic dimension in the ways in which all institutions preserve themselves" (1987, 196) and that ascetic discipline "concentrates on thoughts almost more intently than on behavior" (276). It may be that the particular institution of Christian marriage preserves itself largely by means of an ascetic discipline applied at least as conscientiously to sexual thoughts as to sexual deeds. Therefore it does not seem outrageous to argue that the Christian construction of a monogamous sexual imagination—where adultery occurs "in the heart" of one's thoughts as much as in one's behaviors—has everything to do with understanding both secular and religious objections to pornography.

It has not been unusual for sex therapists and researchers to observe that complaints about unsatisfactory sexual experience are frequently accompanied by evidence of constraints regarding sexual fantasy and that religion often seems to play a role in limiting what a particular client is able or willing to do with his or her sexual imagination. For example, in their 1975 article, "Imagination Training in the Treatment of Sexual Dysfunction," John V. Flowers and Curtis D. Booraem observed that, in most cases where clients had limited sexual fantasy, "there is easily identifiable early training that such fantasy is wrong, bad, etc., usually involving the parents' or later parent-surrogates' moral or religious codes" (50). Many clients in therapy "feel guilty about having sexual fantasies and need the 'permission' and encouragement of the counselor to feel comfortable in doing so" (Wish 1975, 54).

Christian sociologist Herbert J. Miles probably reflected the sentiments of numbers of other Christians when he wrote that "to imagine oneself having sex relations with someone other than one's spouse is a violation of Jesus' words in Matthew 5:28" (1982, 152). Because of their biblical roots in Jesus' discussion of adultery, the moral limitations regarding sexual fantasy have frequently been understood as offering a protective hedge around the marriage relationship. But at what cost?

In a 1977 publication, *Human Sexuality: A Preliminary Study*, the United Church of Christ claimed that pornography "represents a multimillion dollar enterprise that capitalizes on sexual fantasy" (152). This rather unassuming remark connecting an impersonal business in the public market with an intensely private aspect of personal life perhaps understates the potentially troublesome issue of whether pornography may be a constitutional problem within individual Christian practice every bit as much as it is a problem in the culture at large. Catholic moral theologian Andre Guindon, for example, complained that sex researchers commenting on the issue of pornography had not worked closely enough with the topics of "impure thoughts" and sexual fantasies (1977, 245).

Thus, perhaps alongside feminist Kathleen Barry's argument that social reality shapes our fantasy life and that one of the effects of widespread pornography has been "to introduce movies, books, or pictures as the erotic stimulant between two people, thereby reducing the need for people to relate to *each other"* (1984, 213) must be placed an alternative understanding of the genesis of pornographic mental imagery, one more invested in the individual's spontaneous capacity for prurient interest. In this view, pornography is an inevitable product of the human sexual imagination: "if there were no printed pornography, people would simply make it up themselves" (Kronhausen and Kronhausen 1969, 428).

The contemporary feminist—and Christian—hope that a purer form of eroticism might follow the eclipse of pornographic imagery in society, that an eroticism not tormented by intrusive fantasy images might be possible, comes face to face with a Christian ascetic imperative whose history is very long and whose celebration of the chaste imagination and prohibition against the practice of masturbation suggest that the struggle against pornography within has preceded the struggle against pornography without.

The Historical Background

In the story of Jerome, Patristic literature has supplied a classic example of the Christian ascetic tormented by concupiscent fantasies and images. Far from the stimulants of Rome in a lonely desert, Jerome nevertheless found himself, in the words of Elaine Pagels, "surrounded by bands of dancing girls," his mind "burning with desire" (1989, 89). Another ascetic Christian, the Egyptian Anthony, was troubled by vivid sexual fantasies (82). In *The Body and Society: Men, Women, and Sexual Renunciation in Early Christianity*, Peter Brown noted that for Christians in the early centuries "consent to evil thoughts . . . implied a decision to collaborate with other invisible spirits, the demons, whose pervasive presence . . . was registered in the 'heart' in the form of inappropriate images, fantasies, and obsessions" (1988, 167).

According to Charles E. Curran, "the fathers of the Church are practically silent on the simple question of masturbation" (1970, 213). If, in fact, the sexual impulse does not respond when sated, why has such mental astringency characterized Christian practice if proximate satisfactions, in the form of masturbation, are available to satisfy sexual desire? In *The Care of the Self* Michel Foucault observed: "in Western literature—beginning with Christian monasticism—masturbation remains associated with the chimera of the imagination and its dangers" (1988, 140). Sexual asceticism arguably has characterized Christianity, and where masturbation is not an avenue of sexual release, the imagination has remained a primary locus of sexual torment.

The medieval penitential manuals used by priests as guides in the hearing of confessions reflected a meticulous interest in the sins of the imagination and their connection with masturbation. Pierre J. Payer's 1984 study, *Sex and the Penitentials*, provides some of the details. These documents typically discussed sexual lust, distinguished categories of mental sinfulness, and detailed appropriate penances. For example, one of the manuals observed that despite an inability to consummate a sexual act with a woman he has lusted after, the lustful individual "has committed adultery with her in his heart—yet it is in his heart, and not in his body; it is the same sin whether in the heart or in the body, yet the penance is not the same" (48). Examination of another of the penitential manuals reveals that among the reasons a man's practice of masturbation was called "uncleanness" was the complicitous addition of "the touch or sight or memory of a woman" (57). This early historical testimony to the sinfulness of masturbation joined with sexual fantasy, the pornographic within, has a contemporaneity that is almost uncanny.

In *Law, Sex, and Christian Society in Medieval Europe*, historian James Brundage has argued that the themes of masturbation and sexual fantasy were unimportant to either pagan or Christian writers until the fourth and fifth centuries, when "with the rise in popularity and importance of monasticism and Christian asceticism . . . writers on monastic discipline began treating masturbation and sexual fantasies, both conscious and unconscious, as serious moral problems" (1987, 109).

In *Saints & Society*, their study of Western Christendom between 1000 and 1700, Donald Weinstein and Rudolph M. Bell noted that the struggle with concupiscence involved much more than just finding ways to refrain from sexual intercourse and masturbation—"for saints that was relatively easy." The greater difficulty involved "emptying the mind of desire." "In a real sense the whole problem of holy austerity was played out in the effort to cleanse the mind of impurities leaching into it from the body" (1982, 84).

Sexual sins of the imagination are associated with demons in the *Malleus Maleficarum*, a manual for witch hunters which appeared late in the fifteenth century. This work addressed the problem of "interior temptation" and asserted the blameworthiness of devils who were able to "stir up and excite the inner perceptions and humours," bringing quiescent mental ideas to the attention of "the faculties of fancy and imagination, so that such men imagine these things to be true" (Kramer & Sprenger 1971, 50).

According to prominent sex researcher John Money, "From demons to masturbation to pornography, the representation of eroticism and lust in mental imagery and fantasy has continued to be condemned and accused as the cause of degeneracy and depravity, both personal and social" (1985, 173). Money's provocative suggestion that the contemporary "crime of pornography possession" represents a historical recycling of the Christian doctrine of concupiscence offers an alternative to a feminist reading of pornography which sees it as expressing "contempt for human physicality and for women" (Ross 1990, 246). Money's work surely supports an alternative reading of pornography, one which takes the fantasies of pornographic expression to be isomorphic with the tormenting images of physicality which assault those engaged in the rigors of ascetic practice—whether they be eremites in the desert or spouses attempting to will the one pure thing of mental fidelity in conjugal relations.

A Protestant Perspective

The morally problematic connection between the practice of masturbation and the cultivation of sexual fantasy, including pornography, is nowhere more clearly laid out than in *The Mastery of Sex*, by the English Protestant clergyman Leslie Weatherhead. For Weatherhead, masturbation, as a "detached act" involving the "non-biological use of a part of the body for the purpose of obtaining enjoyment," is neither moral or immoral (1942, 125). What makes the act morally problematic is that it is "so rarely, if indeed ever, unaccompanied by mental pictures which the imagination conjures up" and whose source is in "the depths of the unconscious mind" (126). How one chooses to respond to the lure of these pictures determines one's moral culpability. Masturbation becomes sinful only if the sexually stimulating thoughts and images are deliberately entertained by the conscious mind. When a man masturbates he stimulates his imagination to produce "unclean mental pictures." An indulgence in masturbation fueled by the unclean mental pictures produced in the unconscious mind leads to an interest in "pornography" as a vehicle "capable of helping him make unclean mental pictures, which because they increase the sex secretions again induce him to masturbation" (128).

Weatherhead's close scrutiny of the moral dimensions of masturbation and sexual fantasy is by no means out of fashion among theologically conservative Christians today. For example, in *Intimate Deception: Escaping the Trap of Sexual Impurity*, therapist P. Roger Hillerstrom observed that masturbation is "a big question on the minds of most single people" (1989, 62) and suggested that "a good measurement for an individual questioning the rightness or wrongness of masturbation is, Does it promote lust?" (64). Whatever artificially stimulates sexual desire is to be avoided, including "pornographic films or literature" (137). Ken Unger, in *True Sexuality*, also responded to the "difficult question" of masturbation. In cautioning unmarried young people about masturbation, Unger noted that masturbation required fantasizing, and remarked: "it would probably be impossible to so stimulate oneself without indulging lust in one's heart"—and offered Jesus' remarks in Matthew 5:27-28 as the scriptural anchor for his position (1987, 208). John Court, in *Pornography: A Christian Critique*, claimed that men struggling to resist the temptation to marital infidelity may "fall for the substitute of pornographic publications to provide sexual gratification." For Court, Jesus' teachings about "lustful thoughts" make this activity immoral. Individuals need to be alerted to "the dangers of promiscuity expressed in fantasy as well as behavior" (1980, 82).

But stray sexual fantasies are not always to be taken as a clear sign of moral failure. Clifford and Joyce Penner, for example, in *The Gift of Sex: A Christian Guide to Sexual Fulfillment*, have attempted to distinguish between fantasies, which may imply no intention to act, and lust, which "usually has to do with real people in real places" (1981, 338), perhaps in the recognition that many sexual fantasies—like those Weatherhead recognized as arising from a "nonmoral unconsciousness" (1942, 128)—pass through the mind without triggering any lascivious intentions to commit unfaithful mental or physical acts.

A Catholic Perspective

Although sex therapists and some Christian commentators may have conspired unwittingly to lessen the moral condemnation attendant upon the recognition that fantasy is often a promiscuous medium, the transgressive possibilities inherent in the sexual imagination have continued to be troubling. A recent "Dear Abby" column presented a not unusual scenario. A 35-year-old, happily married woman with three children wrote to Abigail VanBuren to report a distressing dream—"so real I thought it had happened"—in which she "had the wildest, most heavenly lovemaking session with a fellow I had a secret longing for in high school." She reported that she had never dated this man, had been sexually faithful to her husband, and that "it never even entered my mind to have sex with anyone else." Embarrassment prevented her from following through with her feeling that she should confess this to her priest. "It all seemed so natural and right in my dream. I didn't feel a bit guilty until I woke up." Abby's response was to credit the "subconscious" with being the source of the dream material and she told "All Shook Up," "[Y]ou are not responsible for your dreams—only your actions . . . . You've nothing to confess. Don't give it another thought."

The contemporary belief that moral guilt should apply only where the will can be held responsible—that sexual pleasures achieved in the world of dreams do not necessarily betray commitments to marital chastity (or to celibacy)—is not as straightforward as it may appear. Only its status as a dream prevented this woman's wild and pleasurable sex with a man other than her husband from meriting severe moral censure. What is not readily apparent in the scenario from the advice column is that, according to Catholic moral reflection on the sexual imagination, there are gradients of moral meaning between unbidden sexual dreams, on the one hand, and sexual fantasies deliberately indulged in for their capacity to generate sexual arousal, on the other.

Pierre J. Payer's *Sex and the Penitentials* provides evidence that sleep was not a time of innocence regarding sexual thoughts. According to Payer, the ascetic context of monastic life was most likely the original location of Church concern with problems of seminal emission—nocturnal "pollutions" which, with or without accompanying sexual thoughts, signaled some physiological pleasure. Payer cites an early Welsh document addressing the case of one "who willfully has become polluted in sleep" and adds: "this text apparently refers to a person who goes to bed wishing that a nocturnal pollution will occur, and perhaps he is considered to be responsible for bringing it on" (1984, 50).

Catholic moral reflection in the second half of our own century has continued the ascetic examination of the contents of the sexual imagination for signs that one's conscious self has colluded in the production of pleasurable images and sensations.

In *Christian Design For Sex*, Joseph Buckley noted that sin occurs not in "the involuntary excitation of the sexual organs" but "if the will purposely dallies with a carnal concupiscence or succumbs to it" (1952, 84-85). "The mere knowledge or even imagination-picture or actual sight of impure actions is not sinful . . . . The sin consists in the *willful approval*, as implied in desire or pleasure, of impure behavior" (47). Theologian Francis J. Connell continued the distinction between sexual arousal and willful consent in his *Outlines of Moral Theology*. Among the conditions required for serious sin must be "full consent of the will to the act visualized as gravely sinful" (1953, 55). It was possible for a person to remain "indifferent" to the wiles of the imagination if he "keep[s] his thoughts set on something good" and also "accompanies this by a brief prayer" (54).

In *The Law of Christ* theologian Bernard Häring argued that the proper ordering of marital life "against disordered desire" involved the presence of "spiritual hygiene in thought and fancy." Chastity and fidelity must be preserved in imagination and thought and the married couple "must spurn the very suggestion that any other man or any other woman would have made a more suitable husband or more desirable wife than the present partner." After all, Jesus himself had singled out lewd looks as being especially evil (1966, 374-376).

In *The Sexual Language*, published in 1977, moral theologian Andre Guindon observed that contemporary Christians were uneasy with the "traditional massive condemnation of interior 'lustful enjoyment'" (224) and suggested that traditional morality "was not sufficiently concerned with the proper structure and functioning of the imagination" (226). For Guindon, the imagination is essential to man's moral life and creates "a distance between the dreamer and his adhesion to the tangible world." "Imaginative space" is what creates the human capacity "for initiative, modification, withdrawal, refusal" (229). However, fantasy taken to extremes functions as a means of escape from others.

Guindon asserted that the realistic setting of human life was far superior to the constructions of the sexual imagination ("'screwing' beautiful and available golden natives on some paradise island") and cautioned that it was harmful escapism when a person "consistently seeks out sexual fantasies and pursues them each time to the point of arousal" (1977, 231, 236). Still, fantasy deserved better treatment in moral reflection, and "facing our fantasies honestly would tell us a lot about ourselves" (235). The clear goal, in Guindon's view, was to "gradually develop the ability to admit sexual fantasies into the range of consciousness while maintaining necessary control so that both sexual escapism and immoral behavior will be avoided" (238).

In *Christian Ethics and Imagination*, Catholic theologian Philip S. Keane has continued the rehabilitation of the sexual imagination. For Keane, the development of "morally appropriate sexual imaginations" is not furthered when the imagination represses all sexual images (1984, 161), and the effort to develop a disciplined sexual imagination must not exclude the recognition of others' sexual attractiveness (162-163). Keane offered an example of how a male might use sexual imagination appropriately in an encounter with a woman to whom he is sexually attracted: "Mrs. (or Sister or Miss) So-and-So is very attractive to me in a sexual sense; were I married to her, sexual communion would be a wonderful human experience" (162).

Catholic reflection might seem to be moving toward a more positive assessment of the imagination and sexual fantasy as part of what makes an individual whole. But as the stilted quality of Keane's confession of sexual pleasure makes clear, there are definite limits. Recent Catholic efforts to reinvigorate the sexual imagination in no way authorize its use in masturbatory reverie perhaps aided by pornography. Certain kinds of sexual excitement continue to be off limits, and the imagination's role in preserving chastity is reaffirmed. Even for Catholic thinkers sympathetic to the role of the imagination in sexual expression, the self-reflexive pleasure of masturbation remains a mutilation of sex, "a trip to nowhere" (Abata 1978, 45-46) and a "self-centered uncreative pleasure [that] is one of the most dehumanizing factors plaguing human existence" (Guindon 1977, 296).

Provocations of the Imagination

The reflections of conservative Protestant and especially Catholic Christians convey a decided dis-ease with the imagination as a location for sexual arousal. Where monogamy is the required context for sexual expression, and celibacy the prescription for the unmarried, any concession to sexual fantasy—whether in the use of pornography or in the indulgence in mental images which may accompany sexual activity—must be morally scrutinized for signs of lust and infidelity. Many Christians, for example, would be unable to affirm a secular assessment of sexual fantasy which saw it as "the rock on which a stable marriage stands, since it permits mental adultery while preserving monogamy" (Slade 1975, 137). In particular, sexual fantasies accompanied by the stirring of the genitals have been perceived as direct threats to the proper ordering of interpersonal relationships outside of marriage.

However, there have been notable exceptions to the restrictive, often negative, assessment of the imagination's limited capacity for faithfulness. For example, in *To a Dancing God*, former theologian Sam Keen wrote: "the healthy imagination creates a visceral connection between the self and other selves" (1970, 153). For Keen, the sacred rests upon the carnal (150), and reverence for the flesh of others is the "categorical imperative issu[ing] from the viscera," which have a "natural sense of the sacred" (153-152). Although liberal Christian thought has offered this more positive assessment of the possibilities of the imagination in conjunction with pleasures of the body—where "the viscera is not separated from the imagination," (153) it has also witnessed to what Paul Tillich called "the ambiguity of creativity and destruction in every pleasure." Writing in the third volume of *Systematic Theology*, Tillich (1963) argued that "no pleasure is harmless," and that it is a "condescension toward the vital life of man" to suggest that a harmonious self-actualization ever replaces "the undecided struggle between the divine and the demonic in every man" (241).

Pornography arguably poses for Christian reflection precisely the kind of dilemma regarding the imagination that is addressed directly by Keen's notion of the "healthy imagination"—where visceral connections between the self and other selves are "sacred," and indirectly by Tillich's recognition that no human self-expressions escape "divine-demonic ambiguity." Presumably the goal of the "healthy" imagination is to construct other selves always as ends and never as means, as persons with dignity and not as objects. But the task of constructing sexual images of others that do not reflect a selfish interest in them as a means to sexual arousal confronts challenges that are philosophical as well as theological: the historical Christian bias against the role of the imagination in sexual arousal also appears center stage in the Western philosophical tradition. In the section of the *Metaphysics of Morals* translated as the *Doctrine of Virtue*, Immanuel Kant wrote: "lust is called *unnatural* if man is aroused to it, not by its real object, but by his imagination of this object, and so in a way contrary to the purpose of the desire, since he himself creates its object." The particular unnatural practice Kant had in mind was masturbation, though "we consider it indecent even to call this vice by its proper name" (1964, 88).

English churchman Leslie Weatherhead's contention that the sinfulness of masturbation would be obliterated if only an individual could masturbate without having to conjure up "unclean mental pictures" (1942, 128) continues to do religious duty in discussions bearing on the evils of pornography. In "Sexual Ethics and the Single Life," Catholic priest Victor Preller observed that a Thomistic assessment of masturbation would recognize that an "ultimate end" was being displaced in the mind of the masturbator in order that he could "fantasize about the sexual use of some human being" (1989, 140).

For other Christian writers, even to fantasize about one's own spouse may be to diminish that person's humanity. In *The Act of Marriage* Tim and Beverly LaHaye said that "fantasizing will often cause a person to 'use' his partner rather than 'love' him or her." The life of thought should be controlled. "If you are married, think only of your wife or husband; if single, force your mind to think pure thoughts about all other people" (1976, 263).

The thematics of the inappropriate imaginative use of others also appear in Roger Scruton's *Sexual Desire: A Moral Philosophy of the Erotic*. In masturbation, according to Scruton, one creates a "compliant world of desire in which unreal objects become the focus of real emotions." When fantasy replaces the real, the other becomes "veiled in substitutes." In an orgasm fueled more by fantasy than by an attempt to engage in the act of love with another, the orgasm becomes "not the possession of another, but the expenditure of energy on his depersonalized body." Fantasies are "private property . . . with no answerability to the other whom I abuse through them" (1986, 345).

But imaginal abuse can be seen from the perspective of the subject as well as the perpetrator. According to Murray S. Davis, in *Smut: Erotic Reality/ Obscene Ideology*, "most people are unaware of the extensive sexual activity in which their image may be engaging." Apart from professional pinup models, "the rest of us would probably be shocked to discover how masturbators are sexually abusing our likenesses, especially since we are often acquainted with them in other contexts" (1983, 142).

Another example of the way in which the sexual fantasies promoted by pornography or masturbation involve an inappropriate use of the images of others comes from Rousas J. Rushdoony's 1974 study, *The Politics of Pornography*. Rushdoony argued that pornography meets a deep religious need of "Everyman" to somehow attain "the raptures and bliss of the cosmic f—" (33). Pornography offers a dream world undisturbed by reality, where the imagination can have free rein (108). However, those who like pornography "prefer their imagination to sexuality." Responsibilities to others in the external world only cramp the possibilities of the pornographic imagination. "Pornography . . . requires the irresponsible use of a person in terms of the imagination" (109).

Christians and Feminists

To make inappropriate imaginal use of other people, particularly to "abuse" the likenesses of others sexually, is certainly part of what the Christian tradition has taken as the subject of its meditations on lust and adultery in the heart. And reflection on the particular sins of the imagination has not been restricted to the work of casuistical theologians but has involved philosophical and other critical reflection as well.

The liberal social consensus that to think a transgressive thought is not to commit a transgressive deed—that fantasies provide grist for psychotherapy but not hard evidence for crimes committed—has not supplanted Christian preoccupation with the struggle for a pure heart in matters of sexuality. That numbers of Christian thinkers and practitioners have found in the imagination an engine of infidelity, a faculty primed for deception and betrayal in the absence of safeguards, is hardly cause for surprise. And that the evils of masturbatory fantasy and its transcriptions as pornography should be keen sources of moral anxiety in the various Christian camps is hardly shocking news.

What *is* striking in the current flurry of arguments about pornography and its relation to the sexual imagination is the apparent similarity between a perduring Christian desire to purge the heart of lust, wherein the fantasy may be every bit as sinful as the palpable deed, and a feminist imaginal asceticism, for which the images of pornography are themselves transgressive acts against women.

In "Toward a Conversation about Sex in Feminism: A Modest Proposal," Carole S. Vance and Ann Barr Snitow argued that some feminists have based their objection to pornography on the grounds that "visual representation or objectification" amounted to literal as well as metaphorical violence (1984, 129). According to Vance and Snitow, important categories of analysis are collapsed when "feelings and acts are not only connected but overconnected." Even private sexual imagery becomes actionable. "Start at the top with male masturbation, which involves fantasy and objectification. Fantasy and objectification have some relationship to pornography, which has a relationship to violent pornography, which has a relationship to rape." If one collapses categories in this manner, "then male masturbation leads to rape" (130).

One need not press the antipornography argument to this extreme to see that its apparent unwillingness to disconnect behavior and fantasy—to allow that consensual behavior and fantasy are not necessarily violent acts (1984, 129)—renders it isomorphic with traditional as well as contemporary Christian attempts to convict the imagination itself of tangible offenses against approved sexual expression.

Though feminists opposed to pornography should not necessarily be identified with the opposition to masturbation displayed by so many Christians who also oppose pornography, even here there is a resemblance in the argumentation. For example, according to Julia Penelope, "to the extent that we rely on fantasies for our masturbation, we have objectified our own sexual feelings" (1980, 102). Her suggestion that "fantasy, as an aspect of sexuality, may be a phallocentric 'need' from which we are not yet free" (103) could easily pass for conservative Christian rhetoric about the need to protect the marriage relationship from imaginal intrusions whose stimulation is sinful.

Writing in *Beyond Domination: New Perspectives on Women and Philosophy*, Eva Feder Kittay claimed that the immorality of "using" another person applies every bit as much to the "image of the individual" as to the individual her- or himself. According to Kittay, "the pleasure derived from the experience of seeing or contemplating or imagining another's victimization involves the exploitative use of the victimized person and her/his pain for one's own interests" (1984, 159). The only morally acceptable pleasures would seem to be those free of any exploitation of others. A feminist sexual ethic concerned to purify the collective sexual imagination—and with particular attention to the masturbators who are sexually abusing the likenesses of women—confronts an ascetic challenge every bit as daunting, and finally unworkable, as one faced by desert monks in the early centuries of Christendom and fixed in perpetuity by never-diminishing numbers of mentally fastidious Christians.

What has been missing from contemporary debates about pornography is sufficient attention to the role Christianity has played in structuring the sexual imagination as a primary location of moral integrity, and consequently of transgression. Feminists seeking to expunge the politically incorrect images of pornography from both mental life and social reality might be surprised, and perhaps affronted, at the suggestion that the religions of patriarchy had anticipated their quest. However, if Murray S. Davis is right, that "the desire to protect the mental image of a person's identity, held by both that person and by others, from the threat of sexually induced disintegration is the prime motivation for the Jehovanist [Judeo-Christian] restrictions against sex" (1983, 122), then certain expressions of feminism owe more to the ideology of Christianity than has heretofore been recognized. Specifically, feminist objections to pornography appear to be homologous to Christian ones in their attempt to restrict, confine, or denature the productions of the sexual imagination in the service of sexuality that is egalitarian (if not necessarily monogamous for some feminists).

It may be argued against this position that not all feminists opposed to pornography are suggesting that the male (or female) sexual imagination is so reprobate that it must be forcibly retired, that sexual fantasy itself must go away. What one sees when one "looks" with his or her mind's eye may make some difference. Yet, the argument against the extremities of the imagination—in its Christian form an expression of the fear that fantasy violates or betrays the marriage covenant, in its feminist form the concern that fantasy trades on inegalitarian and exploitative images of others—must inevitably confront the headstrong confession of the nonsectarian sexual body to its preferred pathway to orgasm. When theologians Beverly Harrison and Carter Heyward wrote that "many people (feminists and others) find it hard to sustain high levels of sexual excitement in the context of friendship," they were indicting patriarchal culture for posing self against other in a tension-producing dichotomy that prevents the structuring of "full eroticization in mutuality" (1989, 162).

Against the hopes of Harrison and Heyward, and those of many other feminists and Christians, for sexual expression that is morally and politically acceptable because fully mutual, must be posed the intractable, and thoroughly Augustinian, problem of sexual excitement that can in principle never be fully mutual and is inevitably self-seeking. The theoretical work of late contemporary psychoanalyst Robert J. Stoller on the dynamics of sexual excitement confirms this theological point.

Chapter 5

The Dynamics of Sexual Excitement:
The Research of Robert J. Stoller, M.D.

In their introduction to *Re-Making Love: The Feminization of Sex*, Barbara Ehrenreich, Elizabeth Hess, and Gloria Jacobs observed that sexual desire "takes strange paths through a landscape of inequality" and that "we need to be able to follow them, at least in spirit, before we judge" (1986, 9). No aspect of human interaction has presented a more intractable challenge to the moral and political aspirations of feminists and Christians alike than the compelling and often vagarious aspects of sexual desire or excitement. Further, the many opponents of pornography, for whom no purportedly inegalitarian sexual practice or its representation in words or images must be allowed to stand uncondemned, have found it extremely difficult to abjure judgment until the inequalities of the sexual landscape have been thoroughly searched and examined.

The quest for equality or parity in sexual practice and its representations has led frequently to a rejection of pornography, because of its perceived unequal and biased treatment of women, and often, though not always, to an affirmation of erotica, whose portrayals of sexual practice announce that one person's sexual pleasures must not come at the expense of another's. Sex between equals rules out exchanges between sexual masters and sexual slaves. This agenda for sexual equality was unmistakable in feminist Gloria Steinem's claim that erotica, as distinct from pornography, "doesn't require us to identify with a conqueror or a victim" (1978, 54). It reappeared in the insistence of The Kensington Ladies' Erotica Society that erotica produced by their members not portray women characters as victims (1984, 223; 1986, 218).

Enter psychoanalyst Robert J. Stoller to claim that in pornography—which for Stoller encompasses all materials manufactured with the intent to produce erotic excitement (1985a, 15)— "there is always a victim, no matter how disguised: no victim, no pornography" (1970, 490). The scripts of men's pornography as well as women's (which Stoller, not alone among researchers, identifies as romance novels) contain themes of hostility. According to Stoller, "for most people most of the time, a touch of cruelty may be a trace element in erotic fantasy" (Colby and Stoller 1988, 147). Women are by no means exempt from his claim that "humans are not a very loving species and that that is especially so when they make love" (1976, 909).

Against the hopes of religious feminists Beverly W. Harrison and Carter Heyward, and others, both secular and religious, with similar sentiments, that "eroticization in mutuality" (1989, 162) rather than an inevitable and conflictual choice between self- and other-enhancement (164) can be the hallmark of satisfying sex must be placed the disturbing work of Robert J. Stoller, whose psychoanalytically informed studies of the dynamics of sexual excitement suggest that the linking of erotic desire or excitement with inequality, which Harrison and Heyward identify as the harmful work of patriarchal culture (150), is, rather, residually intrapsychic, with robust dimensions that render utopian any moral or political attempt to remake sex in the image of equality and friendship (162).

In a chapter intriguingly titled "Sex as Sin" (1975, 207-219), Stoller writes: "In demonstrating that hostility plays an essential role in forming and maintaining human sexual excitement, I was also, subliminally, studying some of the dynamics of ethics and morality" (207). A narrative review of Stoller's research functions to deepen our understanding of the complexities of human sexuality and to confirm the controlling presence of moral issues therein.

Robert J. Stoller, psychoanalyst and professor of psychiatry at UCLA until his tragic death in an automobile accident in September

1991, wrote extensively on gender identity issues, perversion, and sexual excitement. An early article, "Transvestites' Women," examined the connection between the erotic interests of many male transvestites in representations of phallic or cruelly beautiful women and these men's perceptions that the women in their lives who are sexually important possess all the power (1967, 337). According to Stoller, these women—the mothers, sisters, girl friends, and wives—possess in common the "fear of and need to ruin masculinity" (333). The transvestite's desire to dress as a woman, along with the sexual excitement this brings, converts the original humiliation of damaged masculinity into an active process of sexual mastery and pleasure. In feminine disguise, the transvestite male gets his revenge on women (337).

A 1974 book, *Sex and Gender*, dealt with the development of masculinity and femininity—gender identity—from a psychoanalytic perspective and featured clinical studies of patients with and without biological abnormalities. Stoller believes that sex and gender are not coterminous: "one can speak of the male sex or the female sex, but one can also talk about masculinity and femininity and not necessarily be implying anything about anatomy or physiology." For the large areas of behavior, feelings, thoughts, and fantasies that are related to the sexes and yet do not have primarily biological connotations Stoller reserves the term 'gender' (vii). Although he concludes that "those aspects of sexuality that are called gender are primarily culturally determined," or learned, he also believes that the development of gender "is augmented, or interfered with, by certain biological forces" (xi).

Presentations of Gender, published in 1985, is another chapter in Stoller's efforts to find nonbiological roots of gender behavior. In this work he continues to emphasize that the determinants of biological sex—maleness and femaleness—are not what fix unswervingly the psychological state of gender identity, that is, masculinity and femininity. In a chapter on "Biology and Gender Identity" Stoller notes that the resting tissue of all mammals, including humans, is female. In experiments with animals, that are not contradicted by any human studies based on chromosomal disorders, a withholding of androgen, a hormonal compound, during critical times in the course of fetal life means that the "anatomy and behavior typical of that species' males do not occur, regardless of genetic sex." Correlatively, the introduction of androgen at critical times in fetal development means that anatomy and behavior typical of that species' males do occur, regardless of genetic sex. But, as Stoller points out, the roots of human behavior are much more complex than those of animals (1985b, 74), and "in most instances in humans, postnatal experiences can modify and sometimes overpower already present biologic tendencies" (6).

Stoller's interest in the development of masculinity and femininity led to an interest in perversion. A 1970 essay, "Pornography and Perversion," argued that pornography—the erotic daydream translated into words or pictures (490)—is "the highly condensed story of [the perverse subject's] perversion: its historical origins in reality, its elaborations in fantasy, its manifest content which disguises and reveals the latent content" (495-496). What makes the use of pornography technically perverse for the Freudian Stoller is that it indicates a persistent "preference for a genitally stimulating exciting act which is not heterosexual intercourse." At the heart of all perversions, including pornography, is "a fantasied act of revenge" which condenses a life history—memories and fantasies, traumas, frustrations, and joys. The perversion of pornography, which provides restitution for men, comes in different genres, "each created for a specific perverse need by exact attention to detail" and each "defin[ing] an area of excitement that will have no effect on a different man " (490).

According to Stoller, an essential quality of both perversion and pornography is sadism, or revenge for a passively experienced trauma (1970, 495). Thus, for example, the fantasy or act of "poisoning or humiliating one's partner with ejaculate" or of causing physical damage to someone by one's phallic onslaught (495) functions to convert sexual trauma into triumph (494). In this early article, Stoller speculates that the patterns of sexual excitement of nonperverse people may contain mechanisms converting sexual trauma to triumph not unlike those purportedly at work in perversions such as transvestism (494).

How do women figure in Stoller's theorizing here about the function of pornography? They have their own pornography, "but most men have not recognized it as pornographic because it would not excite a man" (1970, 499). Stoller offers as one example of women's pornography romance stories, "where what is emphasized is affection, closeness, courtliness, a little lovely masochism that disguises gentle triumph over a manly man, but not sweating anatomy" (499). Women are culturally perceived as being less voyeuristic than men and thus a less fitting audience for pornography, although social trends in the direction of more exposure of women to (men's) pornography may alter a view that hard-core portrayals of sex are not arousing to women (499).

In 1975 the essay on "Pornography and Perversion" became part of a book Stoller called *Perversion: The Erotic Form of Hatred*. This work gathered together essays on the development of masculinity, homosexuality, the dynamics of perversions, connections between psychoanalytic theory and sex research from other theoretical perspectives, and, particularly salient for the purposes of this study, a chapter called "Sex as Sin."

The examination of the fantasies of the perverse reveals "remnants of the individual's experiences with other people who in the real world, during childhood, provoked the reaction that we call perversion. And at the center is hostility" (1975, 55). Stoller goes on to suggest that "just as every human group has its myth, perhaps for every person there is *the* sexual fantasy (perversion?)." Pornography, then, becomes "the communicated sexual fantasy of a dynamically related group of people" (115), and, consequently, belongs to the normal as well as the clinically perverse. However, to suggest that hostility plays a major role in sexual arousal—that "a need to damage, not love, one's partner" fuels desire—is to run the risk of finding that there is very little, including much of heterosexual behavior, that might not have a touch of the perverse. Freud implies as much in his description of the oedipal conflict and the pitfalls of libidinal development (97). Who, then, are the erotically healthy? As Stoller suggests elsewhere, perhaps only "several" heterosexual and homosexual people (1985a, 102-103), and he claims that it may be more truthful, and less polemical, regarding erotic behavior to assume that most people are abnormal.

In the chapter of *Perversion* entitled "Sex as Sin," Stoller defines sin as the exalted term for the desire to harm others (1975, 207) and argues that the "ruthless possessiveness and destructive urges of early life . . . provide data and a framework essential for understanding the sense of sin" (209). Sin is not likely to disappear when particular cultural-historical configurations have changed. In particular, the sinfulness of sex is perhaps less an artifact of the constraints of Judeo-Christian moral culture than an aspect of the dynamics of sexual pleasure within a person. According to Stoller, feeling sinful about sex comes in part from the (at least faint) awareness "that some of sexual excitement depends on the desire to harm others," and this awareness that one is sinning often increases sexual excitement (208).

All sins are not equal, however. A rape fantasy, for example, is not an act of palpable violence, "and the transvestite's unconscious fantasy of revenge leads to nothing more violent than his masturbating into a lady's hat." Nevertheless, it is foolish, says Stoller, to deny that it is often the hostility and dehumanization in the fantasies that make for sexual excitement (1975, 210). He readily acknowledges that the dehumanization of our sexual objects works against our capacity to love (211), that "unchecked sexuality dehumanizes erotic life and thus thwarts love" (212), and that people would be better off nonperverse (214). However, what Stoller finds missing in arguments that would limit the freedom of press and speech and the right to private perversion is "some demonstration that the mass of mankind is inherently good and that its capacity for love rather than hatred can be harnessed *now*, not in some unstated future" (213).

The third aspect of Stoller's research program, after gender identity issues and perversion, has been sexual excitement. An article entitled "Sexual Excitement" appeared in *Archives of General Psychiatry* in 1976 and reviewed Stoller's ideas of the common denominators in the mind, regardless of culture or era, that "energize" sexual excitement (900). Stoller points out here that different states of subjective experience characterize sexual excitement. An erotic experience for one individual is nonerotic for another. Sexual excitement is, in this subjective sense, idiosyncratic; it involves "scripts" (Gagnon and Simon 1973) that people, in order to get excited, create in their minds (900). Stoller claims that "none but the pornographers have worked the area I am now discussing" (901). Sexual excitement is "best understood if one looks on the process as the unfolding of a scenario written and continually refined throughout one's life." Sexual scripts, which are created to undo frustration, trauma, and intrapsychic conflict (905), and whose resolutions are best celebrated by orgasm (908), by no means belong solely to the clinically perverse but apply as well in the normative world (905).

Regarding future research on sexual excitement, Stoller predicted that "permutations of hostility will be found far more frequently than is acknowledged today." However, he admitted to being less certain "how extensively hostility and its permutations, especially revenge, are found in any episode of sexual excitement" (1976, 908). At the article's conclusion Stoller reminded readers that aggression is not a good substitute word for hostility. Aggression, implying movement or action but not indicating direction, fails to capture the purposeful quality of hostility, which is focused or directed at someone who is to be harmed. If hostility seemed too strong a word for what Stoller was later to call a "trace element" present in erotic fantasy (Colby and Stoller 1988, 147), there was no good substitute ("What is the word for just a whisper of hostility?") to indicate the degree to which sexual pleasure in most humans depends on neurotic mechanisms. For Stoller the "sometimes nonhostile" conditions of love, affection, generosity and concern add to sexual excitement only in rare individuals. "For most people, these last sweet conditions may only threaten one's capacity for gratification and are associated with loss, not increase, of excitement and pleasure" (909).

A 1979 essay, "Centerfold," presented and analyzed transcripts of interviews Stoller had with a woman who poses for soft-core pornography. Here again Stoller's hypothesis is that "erotic daydreams in pornography represent fantasies of revenge in which the consumer imagines he is degrading—dehumanizing—women." According to Stoller, "men fetishize—dehumanize—women in order to be erotically stimulated" (1979a, 1019). The reduction of the full humanness of erotic partners, which is practiced by women as well as men (1019), allows one to master the imagined dangers of intimacy (1024). Critical to Stoller's work on the dynamics of sexual excitement is the recognition that "although sexual excitement is experienced as an automatic, uncomplicated, natural (with implications both of biology and theology) phenomenon, it is actually dense with meanings at all levels of awareness" (1024).

Sexual Excitement: Dynamics of Erotic Life, published in 1979, is a study of a young woman in psychoanalysis whose preferred erotic scenario—"an erotic daydream in which she was being raped by a horse while a group of silent men watched, the performance controlled by a sadistic Director"—condenses the story of her erotic life and states the disguised problem whose solution "Belle" seeks in becoming aroused to this particular sexual fantasy (1979b, xi). A primary hypothesis for Stoller is that everyone has a preferred erotic fantasy (220), and a main purpose of this study "is to show that the same factors, though in differing degrees and with different scripts, are present in excitements labeled perverse and in those considered normal" (xiii). Unfortunately, because too many individuals have perverted their erotism (xiv), scripts for sexual excitement "express for most people the theme of harming one's erotic object in order to get revenge or otherwise undo painful experiences from infancy on" (220).

Hostility, revenge, and the desire to harm are by no means the whole story of the dynamics of sexual excitement, and Stoller admits that much of his work has left "latent" the theme of affection, tenderness, and love (1979b, xiii). Sexual pleasure, he claims, is not diminished by the reduction of hatred that analysis produces. "Instead, erotic activities—excitement and gratification—get more tender. They do not become less forceful or less potent for being less frantic" (222). Over the course of analysis, Belle's prototypic daydream with its thematics of humiliation (68) lost its power to excite her. "Her sexual relations changed, so that she was now able, freely and with erotic feeling, to behave as she had never before permitted herself." Coital orgasms replaced masturbatory ones and "intercourse from behind lost its excitement because she no longer enjoyed its sense of disengagement from another human" (212).

A therapeutically satisfying transformation of Belle's erotic preference for the dynamics of revenge and humiliation into one where the emotional and physical gratifications of "penis-in-vagina intercourse" are accented (1979b, 222) does not directly address the question in what ways women are unlike men in erotic behavior. Stoller presumes that higher levels of androgens in males make for differences in gender and erotic behavior and that androgen levels also contribute to the more "imperious" demand by biology on the erotic behavior of most young men as compared with most young women (220). And what of the influence of culture on the sexualities of men and women? "Do women practice perversions less than men; do women masturbate less than men; do fewer women masturbate than men?" (220). Do men and women differ significantly in areas such as responsiveness to pornography and to visual aspects of sexuality, extent to which hostility is thematic, or capacity and comfort in matters of intimacy and affection? Stoller's response is that we need more data: psychodynamic, cross-cultural, biologic (221).

Observing the Erotic Imagination, published in 1985, continued Stoller's work on the dynamics of erotic behavior with its thesis that the desire to harm or humiliate one's erotic object was present not only in the certifiably perverse but also in the pornographies of everyday life and in the erotic excitement of the nonperverse patients he had been treating for years (1985a, vii). Chapters devoted to clinical studies of rare erotic conditions ("Transvestism in Women," "Erotic Vomiting") and candid observations about psychoanalytic methodology ("I cannot stomach psychoanalytic jargon and rhetoric" [x]) are combined in this work with Stoller's continuing reflections on the role of hostility in sexual excitement.

Here Stoller observes that perversion is the solution to a failure of intimacy and that the nonperverse person does not powerfully fear intimacy. "You realize, then, that at the bottom of my descriptions [of perversion] is a moral, not a scientific issue" (1985a, 43). Because of its themes of trauma, humiliation, revenge, and deception (69), the published daydream that is pornography (21) invites moral scrutiny but also suggests analytical caution. "Only fanatics equate thoughts with deeds." For Stoller the criterion of morality should apply to the actual harming of others and not to fantasies of harming. There is no unbiased data that "nasty thoughts" lead usually to "very nasty acts" (41).

Although the aesthetic experience of erotic excitement does not feel constructed (1985a, 49), its apparent spontaneity is actually "dense" with meanings at all levels of awareness. Sexual excitement is not the automatic, uncomplicated, and natural experience that biology and theology, for example, have supposed. For Stoller, one's sexual excitement can be moved about "like a piece of furniture" (85).

According to Stoller, there is for women as well as men a dark side to erotic excitement. Although he claims that having the fantasy of harming is usually only a small part of one's total erotic experience, the mechanism of hostility survives as "a trace element" (1985a, 42). Significantly, Stoller's psychoanalytic work does not support claims by feminist groups that it is only men's pornography (and mental life) that is rife with themes of hostility. Hostility is thematic, he claims, in the erotic scripts and daydreams of both men and women (68).

That women practice almost none of the official psychiatric diagnoses of perversion complicates attempts to minimize differences between men and women, regardless of how these differences are theorized. Stoller candidly admits that he cannot account for the differences between men and women in perverse behavior, and he does not believe that a social change in the direction of more equal treatment for women is likely to make accessible a range of "women's perversions" that researchers have been previously unable to detect. Nor are women likely to approach the male norm of fetishizing body parts (1985a, 34-35).

Even though Stoller observes that the two groups—men and women—should be seen as two overlapping bell curves, he believes most boys are driven by their erotic physiology more than girls are, the adult psyches of adult males disclosing the shaping influence of the intense erotic need or hormonally-induced urgency of the pubertal years. "Listening to patients in analysis, I hear the urgency of most men's stiff cocks and its contrast with most women's greater capacity, even when excited, to wait, forego, refuse if they feel it appropriate to the meaning of the moment." Certainly women can be "erotically frantic," but this is less a genital need and more likely "erotomania, which is more a fire in the soul than in the perineum" (1985a, 34).

Intimate Communications: Erotics and the Study of Culture (1990), written with ethnographer Gilbert Herdt, brings to the study of a tribe in Papua New Guinea, which Herdt had previously researched alone, the investigative acumen of an anthropologist and a psychoanalytic psychiatrist working together. Stoller had noted previously that data provided by anthropologists were vital to any study of sexual behavior but had lamented the lack of research reports that were other than superficial and opinionated (1973, 249-250). Also, he had cautioned readers of *Sex and Gender* that his research lacked controls from other cultures, the majority of his patients having been white, middle-class Americans, and he noted then that he planned to correct this flaw in the future (1974, xii). Stoller's collaboration with Herdt—the analyst working with the ethnographer—advances the thesis that subjectivity, typically the province of the clinician, is important in studying culture, erotics, and gender identity (Herdt and Stoller 1990, viii). "What the observer feels and what is felt by those whom we observe is part of the research and not an interference to be washed out in research methodology" (ix).

Pain & Passion: A Psychoanalyst Explores the World of S & M, published in 1991, is an ethnographic exploration of sadomasochistic behavior. The major portion of the text is a record of Stoller's conversations with his S & M informants, consensual sadomasochists not very much like one another "except in their powerful commitment to getting erotic pleasure from giving or receiving pain" (1991b, 34). Stoller is curious about the origins of sadomasochistic scripts (24), explores his "etiologic hunch" that severe physical suffering in childhood helps explain the need for S & M (26), and acknowledges a personal change in attitude: "Granting the monstrous deeds that can be committed by those acting nonconsensually, I now think most of the sadomasochistic acts I have listed are, when done by willing partners, not as bad as they seem" (21). For Stoller, the apparent bizarreness of the behavior, despite the presence of pain, is "theatre only" (28), and he thinks we should "distinguish those who harm from whose who, in trying to undo the effects of harm inflicted on them early in life, play at harm" (21).

"Eros and Polis: What Is This Thing Called Love?" appeared posthumously in the *Journal of the American Psychoanalytic Association* in 1991. Here Stoller deals with issues relating to erotic desire from the perspectives of moral philosophy, Marxism, feminism, and psychoanalysis. Religion and science, it seems, have conspired to inflict humankind with a belief in "the normal," which, as Stoller notes, effectively defines what is moral in regard to mental life (1991a, 1072). If it is true that western theology and most analytic theories on erotic desire agree that normal sexual expression is "nonpromiscuous penis-in-vagina" sex, "what most citizens think during normal intercourse would stand a monkey's hair on end" (1074). For the clinician Stoller, any hope that an erotic revolution is possible in which the manifest content of what one sees—the camera record of a woman undressing, for example—is no longer contaminated by fetishizing or by the reconstruction of the object in the viewer's mind "into a different thing, something erotic" (1087), is utopian. Utopian also is the belief in the possibility of nonhostile pornographies (1088).

Although Stoller concedes that we do not know what women's—or men's—sexuality would look like "without the imprint of males' power," he does not share a radical feminist hope that, absent male values, a more harmonious world is possible (1991a, 1091). However, it is true that psychoanalysis has "dodged the truths of sexism" (1097) and needs to acknowledge and confront the presence of unconscious social drives which are political, economic, and cultural (1101). Analysts must change their theories of sexuality to take account of feminist thinking (1096) such as that of Catharine MacKinnon regarding the eroticization of dominance, the maintenance of gender as a social hierarchy, and the preference of professionals for studying female sexuality outside the context of gender inequality and its sexual violence (1099-1100).

The feminists are right, says Stoller: males' pornography does insult women. But it insults men too, making manifest their need to be cruel and marking their failure to relate better to live females. Men, after all, abuse women because they are uncertain, fearful, angry, and envious (1991a, 1092). Although feminists recently have attempted to ground antipornography legislation on the basis that pornography is violence against women, Stoller does not believe pornography is a great threat to womankind (1098) and declares with characteristic straightforwardness: "Drop the rhetoric. You know that rape was not invented by pornography: the designers of pantyhose and the writers of television soaps contribute more to sexism than the X-Rated Industry" (1100).

Robert J. Stoller did not live to see the publication of *Porn: Myths for the Twentieth Century*, a "fragment" from an ongoing piece of urban ethnography (1991c, vii), which records, in transcript form, his conversations with producers, directors, actresses and actors involved in the production of X-rated videos aimed at the heterosexual male consumer. Protected by his "square profession—professor-analyst-psychiatrist—square clothes and demeanor, square-looking office, square life history and private life, and enjoyment of all that squareness" (21), Stoller talked with informants who came to his office to describe their roles in generating sexual excitement.

Producer-performer Bill Margold told Stoller that his reason for being in the adult film industry is, in large measure, to satisfy the desire of the male consumer to see the male porn stars "getting even with the women they couldn't have when they were growing up." According to Margold, when they ejaculate on a woman's face or "somewhat brutalize her sexually," male porn stars are satisfying male viewers' desires to gain revenge against women for remaining beyond reach (1991c, 31). And he acknowledged that adult film industry performers are a masturbatory aid first and foremost (1991c, 61): "you're only as good as the person who's jacking off because of you" (38).

Actress Nina Hartley claimed that performing in adult movies allowed her to help develop parts of her personality, especially socialization skills, that had been stunted in adolescence. She told Stoller she lamented society's fixation on the sexuality of younger, innocent-looking women and its inability to appreciate the mature woman's sexuality: "People still want to see a face on screen who looks like it never even said 'damn,' sucking a cock." (139). Hartley described growing up in Berkeley, which she characterized as the home of radical feminism, antisexism, and anti-objectification. "I fit into that real well. But I was different inside. I was turned on by reading pornography since I first got my hands on it" (140).

Stoller's investigations of the lure of porn for males—which one informant identified as the "fantasy of the blow job," "the one thing the average American guy wants from his woman" but which she will not give him (1991c, 167)—fail to disclose a seamless connection between the formulaic imagery of commercial pornography and the possibilities of sexual satisfaction. Producer-performer Margold, for example, does not perform from erotic desire; instead, he is driven, he claims, by a deflected anger, a rebelliousness aimed originally at his mother (22). And former actress Kay Parker denies that she ever had an orgasm while performing: "For me to climax and orgasm is a very sacred moment that takes time. We never had that kind of time in the movies" (135).

Stoller is candid about the moments that test his investigative equanimity: when the possibility of spreading disease in the adult film industry is minimized; when he and his informants avoid talking about porn's financial relation to crime; when he considers what his response would be if his informants were his own children (1991c, 216).

Stoller's conclusions are sobering. He believes most men, not knowing better, "think that women and men are fundamentally the same in what they want, how to get it, how to express it, and how it expresses itself in our bodies." But the erotic differences are significant. Men, heterosexual and gay, fetishize body parts, are more interested in erotic looking; women, heterosexual and lesbian, look more seriously at personality, are more psychic than anatomical. The problems that energize men's and women's pornography, says Stoller, appear to be "insoluble." "Maybe if the need for orgasm, once excitement is instilled, were always as driven in females as in males or as bearable in males as in females, the two sexes would understand each other better" (1991c, 224-225).

Robert J. Stoller's provocative work on the dynamics of sexual excitement, with its thesis that for most people hostility plays a significant role in erotic life, does not make easy reading for those who believe in the possibility of sex without neurosis, or inequality. Stoller reports that one of his colleagues responded to his theory of sexual excitement by remarking: "I simply cannot believe this explanation! I have *never* felt hostile when excited" (1976, 908). The knowledge that this hypothesized desire to harm another may be hidden as well as overt (903), present in the recesses of unconscious fantasy if not also in the conscious daydreams people tell themselves (901), has not mitigated the severity of Stoller's assessment that "a society's professed ideals of character or anatomy, or other attributes that may be laudable, noble, or saintly"—the reasons we give for loving others—"when sensed unambivalently as worthy, dampen sexual excitement unless they goad one to sully them" (900).

Reviewing Stoller's book *Sexual Excitement* in the feminist journal *Signs*, Robert Michels remarked that Stoller's view of hatred as the primary factor in both sexuality and neurosis is not shared by "most psychoanalysts [who] would see hatred as only one of the many possible contributing themes" (1980, 810). Sex that is perverse, because concerned with healing the wounds and traumas of childhood, is not the only possibility for erotic fulfillment. For Michels, there is the nonperverse situation of "normal" sex (811). And he ends his review by asking, "What constitutes the psychological core of sexual excitement after one attends to the residual narcissistic wounds of childhood?" (812).

In "The Dark Side of Erotic Fantasy," featured in the November 1978 issue of *Human Behavior*, Angela Fox Dunn examined Stoller's thesis concerning the presence of hostility in sexual fantasy. In Stoller's understanding of pornography, "the man looking at the smiling nude thinks all women have been victimizing him, all his life, with their bodies, their superiority. And denying him." Even though the hostility may be hidden, frustrated longing makes people angry (20). Following her presentation of Stoller's thesis, Dunn reviews the work of a number of sex therapists and researchers who modulate or even oppose Stoller's assertion of the centrality of hostility in sexual arousal. Against the essence of Stoller's assertion that "humans are not a very loving species and that that is especially so when they make love" (1976, 909), Dunn offers the views of individuals such as respected therapist Helen Singer Kaplan who maintains that humans are a loving species (21). Dunn disputes Stoller's pessimistic assessment of the virtual ubiquity of hostility in sexual arousal and ends her article by asserting that "loving intimacy is the biggest turn-on of all, but few of us allow ourselves that discovery" (23).

In a 1912 essay, "On the Universal Tendency to Debasement in the Sphere of Love," Freud had written about the difficulties of bringing together affectionate and sensual currents "whose union is necessary to ensure a completely normal attitude in love" (1957, 180). Writing specifically about men, Freud noted: "where they love they do not desire and where they desire they cannot love" (183). For Freud, the tendency to debase one's sexual object, to seek sexual activity with someone "ethically inferior, to whom he need attribute no aesthetic scruples" (185), is a male's particular sexual dilemma. Women, their erotic life also the product of the constraints of culture, experience a condition of forbiddenness regarding sensual activity which Freud thought was "comparable to the need on the part of men to debase their sexual object" (186-87). Love, it seems, never escapes its problematic connection to the genitals. "The instincts of love are hard to educate .... What civilization aims at making out of them seems unattainable except at the price of a sensible loss of pleasure" (189-90).

Despite its apparent pessimism about the possibilities of human goodness, especially in matters of sexuality, Stoller's psychoanalytic work on the dynamics of sexual excitement has had a profound, if unsettling, impact on contemporary conversations about sexuality. The practice of calling into question the scrupulousness of human motivation is not unique to psychoanalysis, however. And Robert J. Stoller's contemporary work confirms an old theological position, linked with the name of Augustine, which has never doubted the human capacity for mendacity, deception, and selfishness—especially when it comes to sex.

Angela Fox Dunn's assertion (above) that the darker aspects of erotic life, such as hostility, do not match the sexual power of loving intimacy, once discovered, conveys an optimism about the possibilities of erotic fulfillment in mutuality. Other contemporary women writers, specifically the authors of *Re-Making Love*, the study of women and sexuality with which we began this chapter, have voiced a suspicion that terms like "loving intimacy" and similar expressions of mutuality in sex may mask a recognition that lovers have different styles and sexual tastes (1986, 100) and that an erotic agenda symbolized by mutual orgasms (99) does not adequately recognize men's and women's distinct sexual needs (100). However, challenging "the old romantic model of sex as an experience of abandonment and self-loss" (100) is not without consequences. Stripped of its *locus operandi* in the mythical couple by a "new notion of separate but equal orgasms" (100), sexual excitement takes on a more idiosyncratic, unrestrained, and possibly deviant cast. There is no assurance that the strange paths taken by sexual desire "through a landscape of inequality" (9) lead eventually to safe terrain where the "full eroticization in mutuality" sought by feminist theologians Harrison and Heyward (1989, 162) can be realized.

Re-Making Love suggested that "for women to insist on pleasure was to assert power" (1986, 196), and it boldly offered sexual pleasure as a legitimate social goal (207). However, there were victims of the sexual revolution of the last two decades—"the women exploited by men's most callous versions of sexual liberation" (202). In the face of evidence that "heterosexual sex" has functioned to assert male domination over women (203), a feminist obligation "to rethink pleasure as a human goal and reclaim it as a human project" was bold, "risky" (208-207). Further, if it was not to deteriorate into silent defeat on the question of what sex could mean to women, the feminist obligation to rethink sexual pleasure would have to abandon the luxury of a puritanical insistence that "every representation of heterosexual sex—however 'soft-core'—is an insult to women and an assault on our rights" (203).

That some representations of heterosexual sex may be an insult to women, and may be designed to be just that, must certainly complicate feminist, as well as dominant Roman Catholic and conservative Christian, agendas for a re-making of love that wishes to preserve the intensities of sexual pleasure while safeguarding the rights of women. Pornography, especially men's pornography with its range of fetishistic interests in the bodies of women, is not readily assimilable for many individuals, both secular and religious, who would speak a positive word for the full potentialities of human sexuality, but who are reluctant to endorse any of the perceived excesses of a disordered interest in women's bodies.

Stoller's work challenges feminist and Christian agendas for sexual expression that is egalitarian. According to Stoller, the paths that sexual desires take, for the normal as well as the clinically perverse, do not readily confirm the controlling interest of love and mutuality in matters of sexual desire. Are men's sexual desires the problem? Stoller's remark that "pornography is, for men, their revenge on women" (1985a, 87) does not authorize an uncomplicated indictment of male, and only male, sexuality for its alleged meanness. In the pornographies of women as well as men "there is always a victim, no matter how disguised" (1970, 490). Stoller's work suggests that an agenda for egalitarian or benign representations or fantasies of sexual activity, where no character is ever the victim of another's selfish quest for erotic pleasure, grossly understates the intimations of inequality—the sin—present in the trajectories of sexual arousal.

Psychoanalyst Robert J. Stoller has suggested that his theory of sexual excitement reflects what others have said for millennia about the difficulties humans have being loving—especially when they make love (1979b, 35). Although Stoller does not write about Augustine, his theoretical work, with its emphasis on the intractably ambiguous moral dimensions of sexual excitement, invites a comparison with this early Christian thinker whose understanding of the intensities of sexual pleasure and their inevitable conflict with more rational interests has left the western world with a decidedly problematic estimation of the role of sexual excitement in human relationships. In elaborating some of the sinfulness of sex from a psychoanalytic perspective, Stoller's work challenges Christians in particular to recognize the selfish trajectory of sexual excitement and to affirm its place in a Christian theological anthropology.

Chapter 6

Pornography's Challenge to Theology

Feminist theologians have recognized that the Christian tradition on sexuality is in need of a thorough revision if it is to speak to the contemporary culture's affirmation of the value of sexual pleasure regardless of relational contexts. *Women and Sexuality*, by Lisa Sowle Cahill, provides a succinct review of the Catholic Christian tradition's understanding of sexuality and identifies some of the directions a feminist revision might take. Christian reflection on sexuality has been shaped decisively by Augustine's deep suspicion of sexual passion and by Aquinas's belief that the physical structure of particular sex acts is the primary determinant of sexual morality. Thus, for Aquinas, "sins which respect the procreative structure of the act are deemed less grievous than those which violate or preclude it, so that contraception, masturbation, homosexuality and bestiality would all be worse than adultery, fornication, incest and rape" (1992, 9-10).

Cahill believes that this theological legacy, with its reluctance to affirm the value of sexual pleasure apart from its role in procreation and its narrow focus on forbidden sexual acts, is deficient. For example, Augustine's anxiety about his inability to bring sexual feelings under rational control may "reflect the male experience of sexual arousal much more than the female." "[R]ecent women's literature on sex and theology centers much less (or not at all) on sexual desire and its culmination in intercourse," perhaps reflecting female sexual experience that is neither as physiologically focused nor as physically uncontrollable as a male's (1992, 60). Thus, to ask, as Peter Gardella did in his study of Christianity and sexual pleasure in America, whether "one day a female Augustine might arise, admitting her own experience in the 'cauldron of lust'" (1985, 160), is to miss Cahill's point that there are significant differences in the "embodied sexuality" of men and women (60).

Feminist theologians and ethicists, according to Cahill, "characteristically establish the context of intimate friendship first, and only afterwards proceed to the question of sexual expression" (1992, 57). In her view, the most fundamental dimension of sex is its relational capacity, and women's sexuality in particular "finds its meaning through the mutuality of partners in sexual desire and fulfillment" (78).

If Cahill is right that feminist theologians and ethicists, presumably Protestant as well as Catholic, "virtually never begin with the fact of sexual acts, then ask after their moral meanings, permissibilities, and limits" (1992, 57), perhaps theological feminism cannot speak helpfully about the significance of pornography in its primary relation to solitary acts of masturbation. Holistic understandings of sex as a relational capacity assume that the deep nature of sexual desire is expressed primarily in paired sexual activity. Philosopher Alan Soble has argued otherwise: "Within a unitary framework, the simple desire for pleasurable sensations is taken as logically primary, even as natural, and the task is to explain both the prevalent paired pattern of sexuality as well as 'deviations' from it" (1991, 156). Short of arguing that, unlike men, women do not use pornography of any kind in masturbation, a feminist theological approach to sex which accents its relational dimensions is limited in what it can say about the spiritual significance of pornography. Catholic writers in particular have to confront official church teaching that masturbation is a grave moral disorder.

Efforts to shift theological reflection on sex toward a more holistic, relational focus run the risk of limiting the church's ability to address the sexual interests many members would confess. Despite the value in taking theological reflection about sex beyond a narrow focus on forbidden sexual acts, it is naive to believe that significant numbers of men and women are not concerned about the moral status of particular sex acts: masturbation, oral sex, anal sex, for example. Can a Christian participate fully and lustfully in these activities? In addition, a focus on the relational possibilities of sex does not provide helpful council for the many who are single, perhaps not involved in relationships, but whose sexual desires are every bit as real as those of married people and possibly find satisfaction in pornography. Men's embodied sexuality, arguably different from women's, typically begins not with the communicative possibilities of sex but with specific sexual acts, in particular, masturbation. And their capacity for prurient sexual interest does not start with their failure to honor the physical and imaginal dimensions of a particular monogamous relationship; rather, it begins well in advance of any expressed interest in paired sexual activity in a boy's engagement with sexual imagery and his recognition of the power it possesses to arouse him physically. Consequently, he defines the pornographic as any imagery to which he can masturbate. If Christianity is to speak to men about the holistic possibilities of sex it cannot afford to drive them into a hypocritical silence about the fantasies that shape their sexual desires.

It has been axiomatic in Jungian psychological circles that an individual cannot become whole without facing and consciously integrating psychic elements which have been excluded or repressed. Becoming conscious of the shadow, or the repressed tendencies of the self, requires considerable moral effort. But a spirit that is not to disown the body must acknowledge the dark aspects of the personality, those nonadaptive parts of the self which possess the ability to add vitality to human existence but whose contributions are thwarted by social conventions (Jung 1983, 90-91). As Murray Stein has pointed out, it was Jung's therapeutic judgment that a primary ailment of the Christian personality involved this repression of the shadow (1985, 153), and many Christians have found in Jung's writing about self-acceptance a vehicle for making the gospel message of healing grace psychologically resonant.

In *Dark Eros: The Imagination of Sadism*, Thomas Moore has brought the insights of archetypal psychology, with its intuitive grasp of the Christian personality and its unrelenting interest in the underworld of the psyche, to bear on the problem of pornography and has explored in rich detail the potential of perverted images to heal the soul. "If we are going to attack pornography," Moore writes, "then we have to deal with the spontaneous pornographic productions of the psyche in nightdream and daydream" (1990, 121). Clients in therapy often reveal dreams and fantasies whose troubling images disturb the moral equanimity of their conscious selves. Beneath the surface personae of morally upright individuals may reside a love of the unseemly, a fascination with the grotesque or sexually perverse, an interest in objects of desire repressed in life. "We know the Sadeian face of human life," says Moore, "but we keep that knowledge to ourselves. Sade had the audacity to go public with secrets usually kept quiet" (134).

The sentimentalizing of sex, with its expectation that everything about it should be personal, is challenged and upset by the genre of pornography, whose profligate imagery expresses a desire to make all sorts of erotic connections, particularly impersonal ones. That pornography never fully satisfies the cravings it expresses makes it a poignant "literature of desire" revealing the direction of the soul's longing (1990, 120). In Moore's view, "the darkest and most perverted haunts of eros have a place in the art of soul-making," and their embrace leads, redemptively, to a restoration of innocence now reunited with its shadow (184).

But Isn't Pornography Harmful?

Those whose erotism resists what is not tender often express an unshakable conviction that pornography, with its images of impersonal sex and its exploitation of women and men, is harmful. Anecdotal evidence, such as convicted killer Ted Bundy's confession of interest in violent pornography, and research studies exploring the effect of sexually violent material on rape have been pressed into service in a campaign to remove the images of pornography from the American cultural landscape. Those Americans convinced that pornography is cancerous are, understandably, unwilling to brook uncertainty when the relation between sexual images and sexual behaviors is on trial. However, even researchers perceived to be sympathetic to the antipornography constituency have issued cautions. Discussing public policy issues at the conclusion of *Pornography: Research Advances and Policy Considerations*, edited with Jennings Bryant, Dolf Zillmann stressed that research on the effects of pornography cannot be definitive; nor can it meet the expectations for rigor and compellingness that have been placed on it: "Not now—and in a free society, not ever. The research leaves us with considerable uncertainty about exposure consequences at the societal level" (1989, 398). Zillmann observed that although researchers have explored in numerous studies the possible connections between sexually violent matter and rape, they have paid considerably less attention to other questions, such as: Does prolonged consumption of pornography lead to increased or decreased sexual satisfaction? Does pornography possibly create "unrealistic, unfulfillable sexual expectations and temptations"? What are the effects of pornography consumption on values concerning family and marriage, as well as on the desire for children (399)?

Following are the opening lines of Alice Walker's short story "Coming Apart:" (1980, 95-96).

> A middle-aged husband comes home after a long day at the office. His wife greets him at the door with the news that dinner is ready. He is grateful. First, however, he must use the bathroom. In the bathroom, sitting on the commode, he opens up the *Jiveboy* magazine he has brought home in his briefcase. There are a couple of Jivemate poses that particularly arouse him. He studies the young women—blonde, perhaps (the national craze), with elastic waists and inviting eyes—and strokes his penis. At the same time, his bowels stir with the desire to defecate. He is in the bathroom a luxurious ten minutes. He emerges spent, relaxed—hungry for dinner.
>
> His wife, using the bathroom later, comes upon the slightly damp magazine. She picks it up with mixed emotions. She is a brownskin woman with black hair and eyes. She looks at the white blondes and brunettes. Will he be thinking of them, she wonders, when he is making love to me?
>
> "Why do you need these?" she asks.
>
> "They mean nothing," he says.
>
> "But they hurt me somehow," she says.
>
> "You are being a) silly, b) a prude, and c) ridiculous," he says. "You know I love you."

For those opposed to it, testimony that pornography is experienced as an intruder in relationships may in the long run build a stronger case against its use than will efforts to secure incontrovertible evidence that pornography is the causal link for sexual crimes. In remarks before the Attorney General's Commission on Pornography, "Evelyn," for example, spoke of her husband's consuming interest in pornography—despite her offer of a loving relationship and the fact that she enjoyed sex with him before he became interested in pornography.

"Masturbation took over our sex life," she told investigators (in Schlafly 1987, 89). And "James," in his late forties and father of four children, told committee members that he struggled daily with "the images, the thoughts, the yearnings, the lusts cultivated during those years of self-indulgence in pornography" (in Schlafly 1987, 146-147). Regardless of the weight one attributes to testimonials such as these, the hurt feelings and the struggle with temptation are real.

However, the core experience of the victimization by pornography may be different for women and men. Whereas men frequently report psychosexual struggles with solitary sexual experience, often in conjunction with explicit sexual materials, women have been acculturated to expect that sexual satisfaction will occur primarily in a relationship, and may experience the images of pornography as graphic displays of interpersonal estrangement. A woman's discomfort with the images of pornography—"Will he be thinking of them when he is making love to me?"—is often compounded by a discomfort with masturbation. Helen Hazen, in *Endless Rapture: Rape, Romance, and the Female Imagination*, writes: "Women agree: masturbating men make them nervous. They don't understand how a photograph can inspire it and, not being subject to the same mode of provocation, can only view the act as inexplicable . . . pornography remains a mystery" (1983, 122). Nancy Friday, in the introductory pages of *Women on Top*, her most recent collection of women's sexual fantasies, writes of her own struggle, as a young woman, to comprehend a lover's desire to masturbate, to be sexual without her even though she was present and available. The rage and fury she experienced at the time at feeling rejected she later viewed as having more to do with her "abrupt realization . . . that he had a life separate from me, was not tied to me in that inextricable way that I was enmeshed with him" (1991, 44). According to Friday, along with an increased experience of autonomy, what masturbation wins for women is a more honest presentation of what it is that excites them sexually (40-41). It may also win them a clearer understanding of the purpose that pornography serves for men: as an aid to masturbation whose depiction of sexual acts excludes extra elements, such as love or more tenderly erotic activity, "because their presence would detract from the true intent" (Hazen 1983, 112).

Pornography's victimization of men is less apparent. Seldom accused of not knowing what excites them sexually, acculturated to bond with other men in creating lives separate from women, men have in recent years come out and confessed, more openly than before, their active interest in pornography. In an edited collection entitled *Men Confront Pornography*, Richard Goldstein writes: "Owning up to arousal by pornography shreds the purdah behind which our imaginations operate" (1990, 82). But the owning up is rich with embarrassment. The man who carries an X-rated movie to the counter of a video rental store may feel the pressing weight of invisible sandwich boards, hanging from both shoulders, whose message, were it visible, would announce to all present: "I masturbate."

Although mass culture uses sex to sell goods to women as well as men, it is arguably the myth of the limitless male libido which fuels and drives the economic appropriation of human sexuality. Mass culture trades effectively on men's subjective sense that sex is scarce, that there is not enough of it to go around, that they seem to want sex more than women do. Pornography, says David Steinberg, addresses "our longings, our unfulfilled desires, the sexual feelings that have power in fantasy precisely because they are unsatisfied in our real lives" (1990, 54). Further, pornography mocks a man's physiological limits, teasing him with more erotic images than he can celebrate by masturbating to, as desire is defeated by refractory periods during which the appetite is blunted and further orgasm or ejaculation is not possible.

Redemptive Possibilities

Pornography deserves to be taken seriously and evaluated carefully—especially by those who may be predisposed to see its various expressions in magazines, movies and X-rated videos, arcades, and phone sex as unforgivable violations of the sacredness of marital intimacy. That pornography speaks a particular truth about the sexual fantasies of many males, if not also of some females, is ignored at great risk by those seeking to formulate a sexual anthropology that is rooted in justice and love, that is egalitarian with respect to gender, and that celebrates sexuality as a gift from God. Advances in visual technologies especially have brought pornography within reach of virtually anyone interested in partaking, and our location in a technologically sophisticated age makes it virtually impossible to preserve a realm of intrapsychic fantasy life untouched by media imagery of whatever type, whether sexual or otherwise. Who can say where erotic imagery is spontaneously generated, as if from one's own undiluted hunger, and where that imagery is stirred, perhaps decisively, by a media culture's largely visual representations of sexuality? Visual technologies exacerbate a male propensity to become what John Berger has called "spectator-owners" of women (1977, 63), the effect of which is to encourage women to see themselves as objects: "Women watch themselves being looked at" (47). However, critics as well as defenders of the genre of pornography are in danger of normalizing its conventions—in heterosexual pornography, the woman who moans at the slightest touch, the man whose erection is huge—and missing the potential of pornography for elucidating the nuances of sexual arousal and their relation to images.

Vox, a recent novel by Nicholson Baker, records an extended erotic phone conversation between a man and a woman, residents of distant cities and strangers to each other, who meet on an adult party line, share sexual histories and fantasies—and climax. Well into the conversation, Jim tells Abby of a personals ad he had composed and whose envisioned encounter he had achieved with a female friend from work. "It said something like, 'You and me are sitting side by side on my couch, watching X-vid, not touching. You are short or tall, etc., you want me to see pleasure transform your features. I am SWM, 29.'" And he proceeds to describe his evening with Emily, the two friends, under a shared blanket, naked but not touching, engaging in "parallel blanket masturbation." He watches her face as she watches the pornographic video, gently touches her arm as she touches herself, and—"the indirect feeling of being able to take the pulse of her masturbating" too much to handle—comes (1992, 98-123).

Baker's construction of this erotic encounter, with its mingling of pornography, masturbation, and tenderness, reprises in a disquieting, but contemporary sexual idiom a familiar, Freudian question: "What does woman want?" Her friend or lover may not know what she wants, may not presume to be able to provide it, may be mistaken in believing that pornography offers trustworthy clues—but wishes all the same to see pleasure transform her features. To call them voyeurs for their curiosity about what excites women sexually, for their interest in watching without directly participating, does not reach the substance of the sexuality, the spirituality, of numbers of men who confess an interest in pornography. And despite its perceived bias in representing primarily what men find sexually exciting, pornography, this artifact of cultures old and new, may function to deepen the sexual connections that are possible between men and women. Pornography can be redemptive, even graceful in its vulgarity—in short, a sign that the spirit is seeking a home in the flesh.

But if pornography is potentially redemptive, it is never fully redeemable, delivered from sin—a wisdom from below brought to the light of day and celebrated. There can be no such thing as Christian pornography, that is, sexually explicit materials which do not turn others into sex objects or somehow exploit them for another's sexual interest. As Susan Sontag has argued, there is something inherently predatory about the act of picture taking itself. "To photograph people is to violate them, by seeing them as they never see themselves, by having knowledge of them they can never have; it turns people into objects that can be symbolically possessed" (1977, 14). At the conclusion of *Theology of Culture*, Christian theologian Paul Tillich observed that making another person into an object is one of the fundamental expressions of sin. According to Tillich, in an industrial society characterized by processes of mechanical production and consumption, no interpersonal encounter can escape this temptation (1959, 210).

The pornographic imagination, which constructs the other as a selfish possession of its own, is arguably constitutive of sexual desire in western culture—an inescapable part of the sin that sex is, whether sanctified by marriage or not. According to Elizabeth Fox-Genovese, "Western Christianity has always had a tendency, well exemplified in Saint Augustine, to believe that sins should be eradicated and judged at their root—in the imagination" (1991, 96). For contemporary cultural discussions of pornography, both secular and religious, the rub comes in asking whether the demonic possibilities of sexuality are ever thoroughly defeated by an ethic of egalitarianism such as feminism has proposed. Camille Paglia, for one, has criticized "Rousseauist psychologies," such as feminism, for their belief in "the ultimate benevolence of human emotion" (1990, 14). For Paglia, and perhaps for psychodynamically informed Christian theology, sex is a dark power never fully free from hostility and aggression. As Paglia says, "Turning people into sex objects is one of the specialties of our species. It will never disappear . . . " (30). A perfectly humane eroticism, free of psychic shadows, may be impossible (4).

The truth made manifest in the graphic clarity of pornographic images is that human sexuality is fraught with meanings other than love and affection. As Stoller's psychoanalytic work has made clear, in an imperfect world neurotic mechanisms such as degradation and hostility which men employ to counter oedipal traumas make sex an unholy descent into the flesh. And, consequently, pornography expresses their revenge against women (1985a, 87). But women's erotic lives too may be driven by a desire for vengeance. Discussing Harlequin romances as mass-produced fantasies for women, Tania Modleski writes: "A great deal of our satisfaction in reading these novels comes, I am convinced, from the elements of a revenge fantasy, from our conviction that the woman is bringing the man to his knees and that all the while he is being so hateful, he is internally grovelling, grovelling, grovelling . . . " (1982, 45).

Feminist Elizabeth Fox-Genovese has argued recently that because men and women are fundamentally different creatures their relationships with each other inevitably will be characterized by at least some mutual hostility (1991, 101). In expressing a male wish for sexual satisfaction at women's expense, men's pornography cuts close to the core of that hostility. Taught by the Christian catechism that sex should express love rather than concupiscence, that endless libido is "a mark of man's estrangement" (Tillich 1957, 54), many Christians of both sexes confront in the commercial and intrapsychic images of pornography a challenge to a more rational conviction that lust is tempered, not lobotomized, by love. Despite their gross failure to represent what many women want from sex, the manifest public pornographies reflect, however dimly, deep human longings for sexual satisfaction whose trajectories are spiritual as well as physical—and need not be confessed in shame.

Bibliography

Abata, Russell. 1978. *Sexual Morality: Guidelines for Today's Catholic*. Liguori, MO: Liguori Publications.

Annon, Jack S. 1976. *Behavioral Treatment of Sexual Problems: Brief Therapy*. Hagerstown, MD: Harper & Row.

Augustine. 1950. *The City of God*. Trans. Marcus Dods. New York: Modern Library.

Baker, Nicholson. 1992. *Vox*. New York: Random.

Barbach, Lonnie, ed. 1984. *Pleasures: Women Write Erotica*. New York: Harper & Row.

_____. 1987. *Erotic Interludes: Tales Told by Women*. New York: Harper & Row.

Barry, Kathleen. 1984. *Female Sexual Slavery*. New York: New York UP.

Benjamin, Jessica. 1980. "The Bonds of Love: Rational Violence and Erotic Domination." *Feminist Studies* 6, no. 1:144-174.

Berger, John. 1977. *Ways of Seeing*. New York: Penguin.

Berry, Patricia. 1982. *Echo's Subtle Body: Contributions to an Archetypal Psychology*. Dallas, TX: Spring.

Blachford, Gregg. 1978/79. "Looking at Pornography." *Screen Education* 29:21-28.

Blakely, Mary Kay. 1985. "Is One Woman's Sexuality Another
Woman's Pornography?" *Ms.* April:37+.

Borden, Lizzie. 1989. Interview. *Feminist Studies* 15:327-345.
By Scott MacDonald.

Bright, Susie. 1989. "Women's Sexual Fiction." *Libido* Spring:13-15.

Brown, Peter. 1988. *The Body and Society: Men, Women and
Sexual Renunciation in Early Christianity.*
New York: Columbia UP.

Brundage, James A. 1984. "Let Me Count the Ways: Canonists and
Theologians Contemplate Coital Positions."
Journal of Medieval History 10:81-93.

_____. 1987. *Law, Sex, and Christian Society in Medieval Europe.*
Chicago: University of Chicago Press.

Buckley, Joseph. 1952. *Christian Design for Sex.* Chicago: Fides.

Bunch, Charlotte. 1980. "Lesbianism and Erotica in Pornographic
America." In *Take Back the Night: Women on Pornography*,
edited by Laura Lederer, 91-94. New York: Morrow.

Butler, Judy. 1982. "Lesbian S & M: The Politics of Dis-Illusion."
In *Against Sadomasochism: A Radical Feminist Analysis*,
edited by Robin Ruth Linden, Darlene R. Pagano,
Diane E. H. Russell, and Susan Leigh Star, 169-175.
East Palo Alto, CA: Frog in the Well Press.

Cahill, Lisa Sowle. 1992. *Women and Sexuality.* New York: Paulist.

Califia, Pat. 1981. "Feminism and Sadomasochism."
Heresies 3, no. 4:30-34.

Callahan, Jean. 1982. "Women and Pornography: Combat in
the Video Zone." *American Film* March:62-63.

Callahan, Sidney Cornelia. 1972. "Sex and the Single Catholic."
In *Sex: Thoughts for Contemporary Christians*, edited by
Michael J. Taylor, 151-168. Garden City, NJ: Doubleday.

Cannon, Ralph A., and Glenn D. Everett. 1958.
"Sex and Smut on the Newsstands." *Christianity Today*
February 17:5-8.

Chapple, Steve, and David Talbot. 1989. *Burning Desires:
Sex in America.* New York: Doubleday.

Chester, Laura, ed. 1988. *Deep Down: The New Sensual Writing
by Women.* Boston: Faber and Faber.

Clark, Lorenne M. G. 1983. "Liberalism and Pornography."
In *Pornography and Censorship*, edited by David Copp and
Susan Wendell, 45-59. Buffalo, NY: Prometheus.

Clement of Alexandria. 1954. "On Marriage." In *The Library of
Christian Classics.* Vol. II: *Alexandrian Christianity*, 40-92.
Trans. John Ernest Leonard Oulton and Henry Chadwick.
Philadelphia: Westminster.

Colby, Kenneth Mark, and Robert J. Stoller. 1988. *Cognitive Science
and Psychoanalysis.* Hillsdale, NJ: Lawrence Erlbaum Associates.

Colman, Barry, ed. 1985. *Sex & the Single Christian:
Candid Conversations.* Ventura, CA: Regal.

Connell, Francis J. 1953. *Outlines of Moral Theology.*
Milwaukee, WI: Bruce.

Court, John H. 1980. *Pornography: A Christian Critique.*
Downers Grove, IL: InterVarsity.

Cowan, Gloria, Carole Lee, Daniella Levy, and Debra Snyder.
1988. "Dominance and Inequality in X-Rated
Videocassettes." *Psychology of Women Quarterly* 12:299-311.

Curran, Charles E. 1970. "Masturbation and Objectively Grave Matter."
In *A New Look at Christian Morality*, 200-221.
Notre Dame, IN: Fides.

Davis, Murray S. 1983. *Smut: Erotic Reality/Obscene Ideology.*
Chicago: University of Chicago Press.

de Beauvoir, Simone. 1971. *The Second Sex.*
Trans. H. M. Parshley. New York: Knopf.

Diamond, Irene. 1980. "Pornography and Repression:
A Reconsideration." *Signs* 5:686-701.

Dimen, Muriel. 1984. "Politically Correct? Politically Incorrect?"
In *Pleasure and Danger: Exploring Female Sexuality*, edited by
Carole S. Vance, 138-148. Boston: Routledge & Kegan Paul.

Dinnerstein, Dorothy. 1976. *The Mermaid and the Minotaur:
Sexual Arrangements and Human Malaise.*
New York: Harper & Row.

Dodson, Betty. 1987. *Sex for One: The Joy of Selfloving.*
New York: Harmony.

Donnerstein, Edward, Daniel Linz, and Steven Penrod. 1987.
*The Question of Pornography: Research Findings and
Policy Implications.* New York: Free Press.

Downs, Donald Alexander. 1989. *The New Politics of Pornography.*
Chicago: University of Chicago Press.

Duggan, Lisa. 1990. "From Instincts to Politics: Writing the History
of Sexuality in the U. S."
Journal of Sex Research 27, no. 1:95-109.

Dunn, Angela Fox. 1978. "The Dark Side of Erotic Fantasy."
Human Behavior November:18-23.

Dworkin, Andrea. 1978. "What Do *You* Think is Erotic?"
Ms. November:56+.

_____. 1980. "For Men, Freedom of Speech; for Women,
Silence Please." In *Take Back the Night: Women on Pornography*,
edited by Laura Lederer, 256-258. New York: Morrow.

_____. 1981. *Pornography: Men Possessing Women.*
New York: Perigee Books.

Dwyer, John C. 1987. *Human Sexuality: A Christian View.*
Kansas City, MO: Sheed & Ward.

Echols, Alice. 1983. "The New Feminism of Yin and Yang."
In *Powers of Desire: The Politics of Sexuality*, edited by
Ann Snitow, Christine Stansell, and Sharon Thompson,
439-459. New York: Monthly Review.

_____. 1984. "The Taming of the Id: Feminist Sexual Politics,
1968-1983." In *Pleasure and Danger: Exploring Female Sexuality*,
edited by Carole S. Vance, 50-72.
Boston: Routledge & Kegan Paul.

Ehrenreich, Barbara, Elizabeth Hess, and Gloria Jacobs. 1982.
"A Report on the Sex Crisis." *Ms*. March:61+.

_____. 1986. *Re-Making Love: The Feminization of Sex*.
New York: Anchor.

Ellis, Albert. 1975. "The Rational-Emotive Approach to Sex Therapy."
Counseling Psychologist 5, no. 1:14-22.

Ellis, Kate. 1984. "I'm Black and Blue from the Rolling Stones and
I'm Not Sure How I Feel about It: Pornography and the Feminist
Imagination." *Socialist Review* 14, nos. 3 & 4:103-125.

Ellison, Carol Rinkleib. 1984. "Harmful Beliefs Affecting the Practice
of Sex Therapy with Women." *Psychotherapy* 21:327-334.

English, Deirdre. 1980. "The Politics of Porn: Can Feminists
Walk the Line?" *Mother Jones* April:20+.

English, Deirdre, Amber Hollibaugh, and Gayle Rubin. 1981.
"Talking Sex: A Conversation on Sexuality and Feminism."
Socialist Review 11, no. 4:43-62.

Faust, Beatrice. 1980. *Women, Sex, and Pornography: A
Controversial Study*. New York: Macmillan.

Ferguson, Ann. 1984. "Sex War: The Debate between Radical
and Libertarian Feminists." *Signs* 10:106-112.

Ferguson, Ann, Jacquelyn N. Zita, and Kathryn Pyne Addelson.
1981. "On 'Compulsory Heterosexuality and Lesbian Existence':
Defining the Issues." *Signs* 7:158-175.

Final Report of the Attorney General's Commission on Pornography.
1986. Nashville, TN: Rutledge Hill.

Flowers, John V., and Curtis D. Booraem. 1975.
"Imagination Training in the Treatment of Sexual Dysfunction."
Counseling Psychologist 5, no. 1:50-51.

Ford, John C., and Gerald Kelly. 1963. *Contemporary Moral Theology*, Vol. 2: *Marriage Questions*. Westminster, MD: Newman.

Fortunata, Jacqueline. 1980. "Masturbation and Women's Sexuality." In *The Philosophy of Sex: Contemporary Readings*, edited by Alan Soble, 389-408. Totowa, NJ:Rowman & Littlefield.

Foucault, Michel. 1988. *The Care of the Self*. Trans. Robert Hurley. New York: Vintage.

Fox-Genovese, Elizabeth. 1991. *Feminism Without Illusions: A Critique of Individualism*. Chapel Hill, NC: University of North Carolina.

Freud, Sigmund. 1957. "On the Universal Tendency to Debasement in the Sphere of Love." In *The Standard Edition of the Complete Psychological Works of Sigmund Freud*, Volume 11:179-190. London: Hogarth.

_____. 1959. "Creative Writers and Day-Dreaming." In *The Standard Edition of the Complete Psychological Works of Sigmund Freud*, Volume 9:143-153. London: Hogarth.

Friday, Nancy. 1991. *Women on Top: How Real Life Has Changed Women's Sexual Fantasies*. New York: Simon and Schuster.

Fuentes, Annette, and Margaret Schrage. 1987. "Deep Inside Porn Stars." *Jump Cut: A Review of Contemporary Media* 32:41-43.

Gagnon, John H., and William Simon. 1973. *Sexual Conduct: The Social Sources of Human Sexuality*. Chicago: Aldine.

Gardella, Peter. 1985. *Innocent Ecstasy: How Christianity Gave America an Ethic of Sexual Pleasure*. New York: Oxford UP.

Gay, Peter. 1984. *The Bourgeois Experience: Victoria to Freud*. Vol. 1: *Education of the Senses*. New York: Oxford UP.

Goldstein, Richard. 1990. "Pornography and Its Discontents." In *Men Confront Pornography*, edited by Michael S. Kimmel, 81-90. New York: Crown.

Goleman, Daniel, and Sherida Bush. 1977. "The Liberation of Sexual Fantasy." *Psychology Today* October:48+.

Gregory of Nazianzus. 1894. "Orations." In *A Select Library of Nicene and Post-Nicene Fathers of the Christian Church* (Second Series), Volume 7, 203-436. New York: Christian Literature Co.

Griffin, Susan. 1981. *Pornography and Silence: Culture's Revenge Against Nature.* New York: Harper & Row.

Gubar, Susan, and Joan Hoff, eds. 1989. *For Adult Users Only: The Dilemma of Violent Pornography.* Bloomington, IN: Indiana UP.

Guindon, Andre. 1977. *The Sexual Language: An Essay in Moral Theology.* Ottawa: University of Ottawa Press.

Häring, Bernard. 1966. *The Law of Christ: Moral Theology for Priests and Laity.* Trans. Edwin G. Kaiser. Westminster, Md: Newman.

Harpham, Geoffrey Galt. 1987. *The Ascetic Imperative in Culture and Criticism.* Chicago: University of Chicago Press.

Harrison, Beverly W., and Carter Heyward. 1989. "Pain and Pleasure: Avoiding the Confusions of Christian Tradition in Feminist Theory." In *Christianity, Patriarchy, and Abuse*, edited by Joanne Carlson Brown and Carole R. Bohn, 148-173. New York: Pilgrim.

Harrison, Beverly Wildung. 1984. "Human Sexuality and Mutuality." In *Christian Feminism: Visions of a New Humanity*, edited by Judith L. Weidman, 141-157. San Francisco: Harper & Row.

Hazen, Helen. 1983. Endless Rapture: Rape, Romance, and the Female Imagination. New York: Scribner's.

Heiman, Julia R. 1975. "Women's Sexual Arousal: The Physiology of Erotica." *Psychology Today* April:91-94.

Heiman, Julia R., and Joseph LoPiccolo. 1988. *Becoming Orgasmic: A Sexual and Personal Growth Program for Women*, Rev. ed. New York: Prentice Hall.

Herdt, Gilbert, and Robert J. Stoller. 1990. *Intimate Communications: Erotics and the Study of Culture.* New York: Columbia UP.

Heyward, Carter. 1989. *Touching Our Strength: The Erotic as Power and the Love of God*. New York: Harper & Row.

Hillerstrom, P. Roger. 1989. *Intimate Deception: Escaping the Trap of Sexual Impurity*. Portland, OR: Multnomah.

Hoff, Joan. 1989. "Why Is There No History of Pornography?" In *For Adult Users Only: The Dilemma of Violent Pornography*, edited by Susan Gubar and Joan Hoff, 17-46. Bloomington, IN: Indiana UP.

Hollender, Marc. H. 1963. "Women's Fantasies During Sexual Intercourse." *Archives of General Psychiatry* 8:102-106.

Hollibaugh, Amber. 1984. "Desire for the Future: Radical Hope in Passion and Pleasure." In *Pleasure and Danger: Exploring Female Sexuality*, edited by Carole S. Vance, 401-410. Boston: Routledge & Kegan Paul.

Hollibaugh, Amber, and Cherrie Moraga. 1981. "What We're Rollin Around in Bed With. Sexual Silences in Feminism: A Conversation toward Ending Them." *Heresies* 3, no. 4:58-62.

Intons-Peterson, Margaret, and Beverly Roskos-Ewoldsen. 1989. "Mitigating the Effects of Violent Pornography." In *For Adult Users Only: The Dilemma of Violent Pornography*, edited by Susan Gubar and Joan Hoff, 218-239. Bloomington, IN: Indiana UP.

Irvine, Janice M. 1990. *Disorders of Desire: Sex and Gender in Modern American Sexology*. Philadelphia: Temple UP.

Issues & Answers: Pornography. n. d. Nashville, TN: Southern Baptist Convention.

John Paul II. 1980. "Lust and Personal Dignity." *Origins* October 23:303-304.

Jung, C. G. 1983. *The Essential Jung*. Selected and Introduced by Anthony Storr. Princeton, NJ: Princeton UP.

Kant, Immanuel. 1964. *The Doctrine of Virtue: Part II of The Metaphysics of Morals*. Trans. Mary J. Gregor. New York: Harper & Row.

Kaplan, E. Ann. 1983. "Is the Gaze Male?" In *Powers of Desire: The Politics of Sexuality*, edited by Ann Snitow, Christine Stansell, and Sharon Thompson, 309-327. New York: Monthly Review.

Kaplan, Helen Singer. 1974. *The New Sex Therapy*. New York: Brunner/Mazel.

Kappeler, Susanne. 1986. *The Pornography of Representation*. Minneapolis, MN: University of Minnesota Press.

Keane, Philip S. 1984. *Christian Ethics and Imagination: A Theological Inquiry*. New York: Paulist.

Keen, Sam. 1970. "The Importance of Being Carnal—Notes for a Visceral Theology." In *To A Dancing God*, 141-160. New York: Harper & Row.

Keller, Catherine. 1985. "Feminism and the Ethic of Inseparability." In *Women's Consciousness, Women's Conscience: A Reader in Feminist Ethics*, edited by Barbara Hilkert Andolsen, Christine E. Gudorf, and Mary D. Pellauer, 251-263. San Francisco: Harper & Row.

Kensington Ladies' Erotica Society. 1984. *Ladies' Own Erotica*. Berkeley, CA: Ten Speed.

_____. 1986. *Look Homeward Erotica*. Berkeley, CA: Ten Speed.

Kinsey, Alfred C., Wardell B. Pomeroy, Clyde E. Martin, and Paul H. Gebhard. 1953. *Sexual Behavior in the Human Female*. Philadelphia: Saunders.

Kittay, Eva Feder. 1984. "Pornography and the Erotics of Domination." In *Beyond Domination: New Perspectives on Women and Philosophy*, edited by Carol C. Gould, 145-174. Totowa, NJ: Rowman & Allanheld.

Kosnik, Anthony. 1977. *Human Sexuality: New Directions in American Catholic Thought*. New York: Paulist.

Kramer, Heinrich, and James Sprenger. 1971. *The Malleus Maleficarum*. Trans. Montague Summers. New York: Dover.

Kronhausen, Phyllis and Eberhard. 1969. *Erotic Fantasies: A Study of the Sexual Imagination.* New York: Grove.

LaHaye, Tim and Beverly. 1976. *The Act of Marriage: The Beauty of Sexual Love.* Grand Rapids, MI: Zondervan.

Lederer, Laura, ed. 1980. *Take Back the Night: Women on Pornography.* New York: Morrow.

Leidholdt, Dorchen. 1984. In "Twelve Vital Voices on the Eighties' Sexiest Debate." *Film Comment* 20, no. 6:29-49.

LeMasters, Carol. 1989. "Unhealthy Uniformities." Rev. of *Weaving the Visions: New Patterns in Feminist Spirituality,* edited by Judith Plaskow and Carol P. Christ. *Women's Review of Books* October:15-16.

Lesage, Julia. 1981. "Women and Pornography." *Jump Cut: A Review of Contemporary Media* 26:46+.

LoPiccolo, Joseph, and W. Charles Lobitz. 1972. "The Role of Masturbation in the Treatment of Orgasmic Dysfunction." *Archives of Sexual Behavior* 2, no. 2:163-171.

Lorde, Audre. 1989. "Uses of the Erotic: The Erotic as Power." In *Weaving the Visions: New Patterns in Feminist Spirituality,* edited by Judith Plaskow and Carol P. Christ, 208-213. San Francisco: Harper & Row.

Loulan, JoAnn. 1988. "Research on the Sex Practices of 1566 Lesbians and the Clinical Applications." In *Women and Sex Therapy,* edited by Ellen Cole and Esther D. Rothblum, 221-234. New York: Haworth.

MacKinnon, Catharine A. 1989. "Sexuality, Pornography, and Method: 'Pleasure under Patriarchy.'" *Ethics* 99:314-346.

Masters, William H., and Virginia E. Johnson. 1966. *Human Sexual Response.* Boston: Little.

_____. 1970. *Human Sexual Inadequacy.* Boston: Little.

Masters, William H., Virginia E. Johnson, and Robert C. Kolodny. 1988. *Masters and Johnson on Sex and Human Loving*. Boston: Little.

Michels, Robert. 1980. Rev. of *Sexual Excitement*, by Robert J. Stoller. *Signs* 5:809-812.

Miles, Herbert J. 1982. *Sexual Happiness in Marriage: A Christian Interpretation of Sexual Adjustment in Marriage*. Grand Rapids, MI: Zondervan

Miles, Margaret R. 1989. *Carnal Knowing: Female Nakedness and Religious Meaning in the Christian West*. Boston: Beacon.

Millett, Kate. 1978. "What Do *You* Think Is Erotic?" *Ms*. November:56+.

Miner, Valerie. 1981. "Fantasies and Nightmares: The Red-Blooded Media." *Jump Cut* 26:48-50.

Modleski, Tania. 1982. *Loving with a Vengeance: Mass-Produced Fantasies for Women*. New York: Routledge.

Money, John. 1985. *The Destroying Angel: Sex, Fitness & Food in the Legacy of Degeneracy Theory, Graham Crackers, Kellogg's Corn Flakes & American Health History*. Buffalo, NY: Prometheus.

Moore, Thomas. 1990. *Dark Eros: The Imagination of Sadism*. Dallas, TX: Spring.

Morgan, Robin. 1977. *Going Too Far: The Personal Chronicle of a Feminist*. New York: Random House.

_____. 1978. "How to Run the Pornographers out of Town." *Ms*. November:55+.

_____. 1982. "The Politics of Sado-Masochistic Fantasies." In *Against Sadomasochism: A Radical Feminist Analysis*, edited by Robin Ruth Linden, Darlene R. Pagano, Diana E. H. Russell, and Susan Leigh Star, 109-123. East Palo Alto, CA: Frog in the Well Press.

Mulvey, Laura. 1985. "Visual Pleasure and Narrative Cinema."
    In *Movies and Methods: Volume 2*, edited by Bill Nichols,
    303-315. Berkeley, CA: University of California Press.

Myers, Kathy. 1982. "Towards a Feminist Erotica."
    Camerawork March:14+.

Nelson, James B. 1978. *Embodiment: An Approach to Sexuality and
    Christian Theology*. Minneapolis, MN: Augsburg.

_____. 1983. *Between Two Gardens: Reflections on Sexuality and
    Religious Experience*. New York: Pilgrim.

Newton, Esther, and Shirley Walton. 1984. "The Misunderstanding:
    Toward a More Precise Sexual Vocabulary."
    In *Pleasure and Danger: Exploring Female Sexuality*, edited by
    Carole S. Vance, 242-250. Boston: Routledge & Kegan Paul.

Nin, Anais. 1977. *Delta of Venus: Erotica by Anais Nin*.
    New York: Harcourt.

O'Driscoll, Sally. 1981. "Andrea Dworkin: Guilt Without Sex."
    Rev. of *Pornography: Men Possessing Women*,
    by Andrea Dworkin. *Village Voice* July 15-21:34.

Offit, Avodah K. 1981. *Night Thoughts: Reflections of a Sex
    Therapist*. New York: Congdon & Weed.

Oraison, Marc. 1958. *Man and Wife: The Physical and Spiritual
    Foundations of Marriage*. Trans. Andre Humbert.
    New York: Macmillan.

Orlando, Lisa. 1982. "Bad Girls and 'Good' Politics."
    Village Voice Literary Supplement 13:1+.

Pagels, Elaine. 1989. *Adam, Eve, and the Serpent*. New York: Vintage.

Paglia, Camille. 1990. *Sexual Personae: Art and Decadence from
    Nefertiti to Emily Dickinson*. New Haven, CT: Yale UP.

Pajakowska, Claire. 1980. "Imagistic Representation and the Status of
    the Image in Pornography." *Cine-Tracts* 3, no. 3:13-23.

Pally, Marcia. 1985. "Object of the Game."
    Film Comment 21, no. 3:68-73.

Payer, Pierre J. 1984. *Sex and the Penitentials.*
Toronto: University of Toronto Press.

Pellauer, Mary. 1987. "Pornography: An Agenda for the Churches."
Christian Century July 29-August 5:651-655.

Penelope, Julia. 1980. "And Now for the Hard Questions . . . "
Rev. of *A Woman's Touch*, edited by Cedar and Nelly.
Sinister Wisdom Fall:99-104.

Penner, Clifford and Joyce. 1981. *The Gift of Sex: A Christian Guide
to Sexual Fulfillment.* Dallas: Word.

Pickard, Christine. 1982. "A Perspective on Female Responses to
Sexual Material." In *The Influence of Pornography on Behavior*,
edited by Maurice Yaffe and Edward C. Nelson, 91-117.
New York: Academic Press.

Pornography: Far from the Song of Songs. 1988. Louisville, KY:
Presbyterian Church (U.S.A.).

Preller, Victor. 1989. "Sexual Ethics and the Single Life."
In *Men and Women: Sexual Ethics in Turbulent Times*,
edited by Philip Turner, 116-146. Cambridge, MA: Cowley.

The Report of the Commission on Obscenity and Pornography.
1970. New York: Bantam.

Report on the Multi-Billion Dollar Traffic in Pornography.
1987. New York: Morality in Media.

Rice, F. Philip. 1978. *Sexual Problems in Marriage: Help from a
Christian Counselor.* Philadelphia: Westminster.

Rich, Adrienne. 1980. "Compulsory Heterosexuality and Lesbian
Existence." *Signs* 5:631-660.

Rich, B. Ruby. 1982. "Anti-Porn: Soft Issue, Hard World."
Village Voice July 20:1+.

_____. 1986. "Feminism and Sexuality in the 1980s."
Feminist Studies 12:525-561.

Robinson, Paul. 1989. *The Modernization of Sex: Havelock Ellis,
Alfred Kinsey, William Masters and Virginia Johnson.*
Ithaca, NY: Cornell UP.

Ross, Mary Ellen. 1987. "The Ethical Limitations of Autonomy:
A Critique of the Moral Vision of Psychological Man."
In *Embodied Love: Sensuality and Relationship as Feminist
Values,* edited by Paula M. Cooey, Sharon A. Farmer, and
Mary Ellen Ross, 151-168. San Francisco: Harper & Row.

_____. 1990. "Censorship or Education? Feminist Views on
Pornography." *Christian Century* March 7:244-246.

Rubin, Gayle. 1984. "Thinking Sex: Notes for a Radical Theory of the
Politics of Sexuality." In *Pleasure and Danger: Exploring Female
Sexuality,* edited by Carole S. Vance, 267-319.
Boston: Routledge & Kegan Paul.

Rushdoony, Rousas J. 1974. *The Politics of Pornography.*
New Rochelle, NY: Arlington House.

Russ, Joanna. 1987. "Pornography and the Doubleness of Sex for
Women." *Jump Cut* 32:38-41.

Russell, Diana E. H. 1980. "Pornography and Violence: What Does the
New Research Say?" In *Take Back the Night: Women on
Pornography,* edited by Laura Lederer, 218-238.
New York: Morrow.

Russell, Diana E. H., and Laura Lederer. 1980. "Questions We Get
Asked Most Often." In *Take Back the Night: Women on
Pornography,* edited by Laura Lederer, 23-29. New York: Morrow.

Schlafly, Phyllis, ed. 1987. *Pornography's Victims.*
Westchester, IL: Crossway Books.

Scruton, Roger. 1986. *Sexual Desire: A Moral Philosophy of the
Erotic.* New York: Free Press.

Shainess, Natalie, and Harold Greenwald. 1971. "Debate: Are Fantasies
during Sexual Relations a Sign of Difficulty?"
Sexual Behavior May:38-54.

Shanor, Karen. 1977. *The Fantasy Files: A Study of the Sexual Fantasies of Contemporary Women.* New York: Dial.

Sherrard, Philip. 1976. *Christianity and Eros: Essays on the Theme of Sexual Love.* London: SPCK.

Shulman, Alix Kates. 1980. "Sex and Power: Sexual Bases of Radical Feminism." *Signs* 5:590-604.

Slade, Joseph P. 1975. "Pornographic Theatres off Times Square." In *The Pornography Controversy: Changing Moral Standards in American Life*, edited by Ray C. Rist, 119-139. New Brunswick, NJ: Transaction.

Small, Dwight Hervey. 1974. *Christian: Celebrate Your Sexuality.* Old Tappan, NJ: Revell.

Smedes, Lewis B. 1976. *Sex for Christians: The Limits and Liberties of Sexual Living.* Grand Rapids, MI: Eerdmans.

Snitow, Ann Barr. 1979. "Mass Market Romance: Pornography for Women is Different." *Radical History Review* 20:141-161.

Snitow, Ann, Christine Stansell, and Sharon Thompson, eds. 1983. *Powers of Desire: The Politics of Sexuality.* New York: Monthly Review.

Soble, Alan. 1991. "Masturbation and Sexual Philosophy." In *The Philosophy of Sex: Contemporary Readings*, edited by Alan Soble, 133-157. Savage, MD: Rowman & Littlefield.

Sontag, Susan. 1969. "The Pornographic Imagination." In *Styles of Radical Will*, 35-73. New York: Farrar.

_____. 1977. *On Photography.* New York: Farrar.

Stein, Murray. 1985. *Jung's Treatment of Christianity: The Psychotherapy of a Religious Tradition.* Wilmette, IL: Chiron.

Steinberg, David. 1990. "The Roots of Pornography." In *Men Confront Pornography*, edited by Michael S. Kimmel, 54-59. New York: Crown.

Steinem, Gloria. 1978. "Erotica and Pornography: A Clear and Present Difference." *Ms.* November:53+.

Bibliography

Stern, Lesley. 1982. "The Body As Evidence: A Critical   Review of
the Pornography Problematic." *Screen* 23, no. 5:n. pag.

Stoller, Robert J. 1967. "Transvestites' Women." *American Journal of
Psychiatry* 124:333-339.

_____. 1970. "Pornography and Perversion." *Archives of General
Psychiatry* 22:490-499.

_____. 1973. "Overview: The Impact of New Advances in Sex
Research on Psychoanalytic Theory." *American Journal of
Psychiatry* 130:241-251.

_____. 1974. *Sex and Gender*. Vol. 1: *The Development of
Masculinity and Femininity*. New York: Jason Aronson.

_____. 1975. *Perversion: The Erotic Form of Hatred*.
New York: Delta.

_____. 1976. "Sexual Excitement." *Archives of General Psychiatry*
33:899-909.

_____. 1979a. "Centerfold: An Essay on Excitement."
Archives of General Psychiatry 36:1019-1024.

_____. 1979b. *Sexual Excitement: Dynamics of Erotic Life*.
New York: Pantheon.

_____. 1985a. *Observing the Erotic Imagination*.
New Haven, CT: Yale UP.

_____. 1985b. *Presentations of Gender*. New Haven, CT: Yale UP.

_____. 1991a. "Eros and Polis: What Is This Thing Called Love?"
Journal of the American Psychoanalytic Association
39:1065-1102.

_____. 1991b. *Pain & Passion: A Psychoanalyst Explores the
World of S & M*. New York: Plenum.

_____. 1991c. *Porn: Myths for the Twentieth Century*.
New Haven, CT: Yale UP.

Suenens, Leon Joseph. 1963. *Love and Control: The Contemporary
Problem*. Westminster, MD: Newman.

Suleiman, Susan Rubin. 1986. "Pornography, Transgression, and the
     Avante-Garde: Bataille's STORY OF THE EYE."
     In *The Poetics of Gender*, edited by Nancy K. Miller, 117-136.
     New York: Columbia UP.

Thornton, Louise, Jan Sturtevant, and Amber Coverdale Sumrall, eds.
     1989. *Touching Fire: Erotic Writings by Women.*
     New York: Carroll & Graf.

Tiefer, Leonore. 1988. "A Feminist Critique of the Sexual Dysfunction
     Nomenclature." In *Women and Sex Therapy*, edited by Ellen Cole
     and Esther D. Rothblum, 5-21. New York: Haworth.

Tillich, Paul. 1957. *Systematic Theology.* Vol. 2.
     Chicago: University of Chicago Press.

_____. 1959. *Theology of Culture.* New York: Oxford UP.

_____. 1963. *Systematic Theology.* Vol. 3.
     Chicago: University of Chicago Press.

Tong, Rosemarie. 1982. "Feminism, Pornography and Censorship."
     Social Theory and Practice 8, no. 1:1-17.

Unger, Ken. 1987. *True Sexuality.* Wheaton, IL: Tyndale.

The United Church of Christ. 1977. *Human Sexuality: A
     Preliminary Study.* New York: United Church Press.

Valverde, Mariana. 1989. "Beyond Gender Dangers and Private
     Pleasures: Theory and Ethics in the Sex Debates."
     Feminist Studies 15:237-254.

Vance, Carole S. 1984. "Pleasure and Danger: Toward a Politics of
     Sexuality." In *Pleasure and Danger: Exploring Female Sexuality*,
     edited by Carole S. Vance, 1-27. Boston: Routledge & Kegan Paul.

_____. 1986. "The Meese Commission on the Road."
     Nation August 2/9:1+.

Vance, Carole S., and Ann Barr Snitow. 1984. "Toward a Conversation
     about Sex in Feminism: A Modest Proposal." *Signs* 10:126-135.

Wagner, Sally Roesch. 1982. "Pornography and the Sexual Revolution: The Backlash of Sadomasochism." In *Against Sadomasochism: A Radical Feminist Analysis*, edited by Robin Ruth Linden, Darlene R. Pagano, Diana E. H. Russell, and Susan Leigh Star, 23-44. East Palo Alto, CA: Frog in the Well.

Wakefield, Jerome C. 1987. "The Semantics of Success: Do Masturbation Exercises Lead to Partner Orgasm?" *Journal of Sex & Marital Therapy* 13, no. 1:3-14.

Walker, Alice. 1978. "What Do *You* Think Is Erotic?" *Ms.* November:56+.

_____. 1980. "Coming Apart." In *Take Back the Night: Women on Pornography*, edited by Laura Lederer, 95-104. New York: William Morrow.

Weatherhead, Leslie D. 1942. *The Mastery of Sex through Psychology and Religion*. New York: Macmillan.

Weaver, Mary Jo. 1989. "Pornography and the Religious Imagination." In *For Adult Users Only: The Dilemma of Violent Pornography*, edited by Susan Gubar and Joan Hoff, 68-86. Bloomington, IN: Indiana UP.

Webster, Paula. 1981. "Pornography and Pleasure." *Heresies* 3, no. 4:48-51.

_____. 1984. "The Forbidden: Eroticism and Taboo." In *Pleasure and Danger: Exploring Female Sexuality*, edited by Carole S. Vance, 385-398.

Weene, Seph. 1981. "Venus." *Heresies* 3, no. 4:36-38.

Weinstein, Donald, and Rudolph M. Bell. 1982. *Saints & Society: The Two Worlds of Western Christendom, 1000- 1700*. Chicago: University of Chicago Press.

Weir, Lorna, and Leo Casey. 1984. "Subverting Power in Sexuality." *Socialist Review* 14, nos. 3 & 4:139-157.

Wendell, Susan. 1983. "Pornography and Freedom of Expression." In *Pornography and Censorship*, edited by David Copp and Susan Wendell, 167-183. Buffalo, NY: Prometheus.

Whisler, Sandra M. 1981. "The Celibacy Letters."
Heresies 3, No. 4:26-28.

Williams, Linda. 1989. *Hard Core: Power, Pleasure, and the "Frenzy of the Visible"*.
Berkeley, CA: University of California Press.

Willis, Ellen. 1979. Editorial. *Village Voice* October 15:8.

_____. 1981. "Lust Horizons. Is the Women's Movement Pro-Sex?" *Village Voice* June 17-23:1+.

_____. 1982. "Toward a Feminist Sexual Revolution."
Social Text no. 6:3-21.

Wish, Peter A. 1975. "The Use of Imagery-Based Techniques in the Treatment of Sexual Dysfunction."
Counseling Psychologist 5, no. 1:52-55.

Zillmann, Dolf, and Jennings Bryant. 1989. *Pornography: Research Advances and Policy Considerations*.
Hillsdale, NJ: Lawrence Erlbaum Associates.

Readings for Further Study

PORNOGRAPHY

Research and Public Policy

Edward Donnerstein, Daniel Linz, and Steven Penrod. 1987.
*The Question of Pornography: Research Findings and Policy
Implications*. New York: The Free Press.

Dolf Zillmann and Jennings Bryant, editors. 1989. *Pornography:
Research Advances and Policy Considerations*. Hillsdale, NJ:
Lawrence Erlbaum Associates.

Daniel Linz, Edward Donnerstein, and Steven Penrod. 1987. "The
Findings and Recommendations of the Attorney General's
Commission on Pornography: Do the Psychological 'Facts' Fit
the Political Fury?" *American Psychologist* 42, no. 10:946-953.

Terry Teachout. 1987. "The Pornography Report That Never Was."
Commentary 84, No. 2:51-57.

Barry W. Lynn. 1986. "The New Pornography Commission: Slouching
Toward Censorship." *Siecus* Report 14, no. 5:1-6.

Carole S. Vance. 1986. "The Meese Commission on the Road."
The Nation August 2/9:1+.

Philip Nobile and Eric Nadler. 1986. *United States of America
vs. Sex*. New York: Minotaur Press, Ltd.

Donna Turley. 1986. "The Feminist Debate on Pornography: An
Unorthodox Interpretation." *Socialist Review* 16, nos. 3-4:81-96.

The Early Liberal Defense

D. H. Lawrence. 1953. "Pornography and obscenity." In *D. H.
Lawrence: Sex, Literature and Censorship*, edited by Harry T.
Moore, 69-88. New York: Twayne.

Susan Sontag. 1969. "The Pornographic Imagination." In *Styles
of Radical Will*, 35-73. New York: Farrar.

Paul Goodman. 1970. "Pornography, Art, and Censorship." In
Perspectives on Pornography, edited by Douglas A. Hughes,
42-60. New York: St. Martin's.

Kenneth Tynan. 1970. "Dirty Books Can Stay." In *Perspectives
on Pornography*, edited by Douglas A. Hughes, 109-121.

Recent Studies

Walter Kendrick. 1988. *The Secret Museum: Pornography in Modern
Culture*. New York: Penguin.

F. M. Christensen.1990. *Pornography: The Other Side*. New York:
Praeger.

Richard S. Randall. 1989. *Freedom and Taboo: Pornography and
the Politics of a Self Divided*. Berkeley, CA: University
of California Press.

Gordon Hawkins and Franklin E. Zimring. 1988. *Pornography in a
Free Society*. New York: Cambridge UP.

Alan Soble. 1986. *Pornography: Marxism, Feminism, and the
Future of Sexuality*. New Haven, CT: Yale UP.

Donald Alexander Downs. 1989. *The New Politics of Pornography*.
Chicago: University of Chicago Press.

Susan G. Cole. 1989. *Pornography and the Sex Crisis*. Toronto:
Amanita.

Linda Williams. 1989. *Hard Core: Power, Pleasure, and the "Frenzy of
the Visible"*. Berkeley, CA: University of California Press.

Robert J. Stoller. 1991. *Porn: Myths for the Twentieth Century*.
New Haven, CT: Yale UP.

Michael S. Kimmel, editor. 1990. *Men Confront Pornography*.
New York: Crown.

The Genre: Venue, Production and Participation

Jerry Butler. 1989. *Raw Talent*. Buffalo, NY: Prometheus.

Linda Loveless and Mike McGrady. 1980. *Ordeal*. New York:
Berkeley.

Henry Schipper. 1980. "Filthy Lucre: A Tour of America's Most
Profitable Frontier." *Mother Jones* April:31+.

Nina Hartley. 1987. "Confessions of a Feminist Porno Star."
In *Sex Work: Writings by Women in the Sex Industry*, edited
by Frederique Delacoste and Priscilla Alexander, 142-144.
Pittsburgh, PA: Cleis Press.

Scott MacDonald. 1983. "Confessions of a Feminist Porn
Watcher." *Film Quarterly* 36, no. 3:10-17.

Joseph P. Slade. 1975. "Pornographic Theaters Off Times Square."
In *The Pornography Controversy: Changing Moral Standards in
American Life*, edited by Ray C. Rist, 119-139.
New Brunswick, NJ: Transaction.

Joseph P. Slade. 1975. "Recent Trends in Pornographic Films."
Society September/October:77-84.

Burton Wohl. 1976. "The Reluctant Pornographer." *Harper's*
December:91-94.

James Poett. 1978. "Deep Peep." *Village Voice* May 1:1+.

Kenneth Turan and Stephen F. Zito. 1974. "Hard-Core Stars:
Two Interviews." In *Sinema: American Pornographic Films And
The People Who Make Them*, 172-187. New York: Praeger.

Robert H. Rimmer. 1991. *The X-Rated Videotape Guide II*.
Buffalo, NY: Prometheus.

Women and Pornography

Kate Ellis, Nan D. Hunter, Beth Jaker, Barbara O'Dair, and Abby
    Talmer. 1988. *Caught Looking: Feminism, Pornography, and
    Censorship.* Seattle: Real Comet Press.

Lois Gould. 1975. "Pornography for Women." *New York Times
    Magazine.* March 2:10+.

Lynne Segal. 1983. "Sensual uncertainty, or Why the Clitoris is not
    enough." In *Sex & Love: New thoughts on old contradictions*,
    edited by Sue Cartledge & Joanna Ryan, 30- 47.
    London: Women's Press.

Lynne Segal. 1990. "Changing Masculinities: Rape, Pornography."
    Continuum 1, no. 1:153-170.

Marion Bower. 1986. "Daring to Speak Its Name: The Relationship
    of Women to Pornography." *Feminist Review* 24, 40-55.

Kathy Myers. 1982. "Towards a Feminist Erotica." *Camerawork*
    March:14+.

Julia Lesage. 1981. "Women and Pornography." *Jump Cut* 26:46+.

Louise J. Kaplan. 1991. "For Female Eyes Only." In *Female
    Perversions: The Temptations of Emma Bovary*, 321-361.
    New York: Doubleday.

Elizabeth Fox-Genovese. 1991. "Pornography and Individual
    Rights." In *Femiminism Without Illusions: A Critique of
    Individualism*, 87-111. Chapel Hill, NC: University of
    North Carolina Press.

Linda Williams. 1989. "Sequels and Re-Visions." In *Hard Core*,
    229-264. Berkeley, CA: University of California Press.

Steve Chapple and David Talbot. 1989. "Pandora's Mirror: The Rise of
    Fem Porn." In *Burning Desires: Sex in America*, 248-296.
    New York: Doubleday.

Laura Fraser. 1990. "Nasty Girls." *Mother Jones*
    February/March:32+.

Sallie Tisdale. 1992. "Talk Dirty to Me: A woman's taste for
pornography." *Harper's* February:37-46.

Gay and Lesbian Issues

Richard Dyer. 1985. "Coming to Terms: Male Gay Porn."
Jump Cut 30:27-29.

Tom Waugh. 1985. "Gay vs. Straight: Men's Pornography."
Jump Cut 30:30-34.

Cindy Patton. 1988. "The Cum Shot: 3 Takes on Lesbian and Gay
Sexuality." *Out/Look* Fall:72-77.

Bibliographies

Betty-Carol Sellen and Patricia A. Young. 1987. *Feminists,
Pornography, & the Law: An Annotated Bibliography of Conflict,
1970-1986.* Hamden, CT: Library Professional Publications.

Gina Marchetti. 1981. "Readings on Women and Pornography:
An Annotated Working Bibiography." *Jump Cut* 26:56-60.

Bonnelle Strickling, with David Copp and Susan Wendell. 1983.
"Selected Bibliography of Academic and Popular Philosophy"
and "Selected Bibliography of Social Scientific Essays" in
Pornography and Censorship, edited by David Copp and Susan
Wendell, 207-210 and 311-321. Buffalo, NY: Prometheus.

Moral Judgment and Religious Responses

Tom Minnery, editor. 1987. *Pornography: A Human Tragedy.*
Wheaton, IL: Living Books.

Reisman, Judith. 1991. *"Soft Porn" Plays Hardball: Its Tragic
Effects on Women, Children & the Family.* Lafayette, LA:
Huntington House.

Jerry R. Kirk. 1985. *The Mind Polluters.* Nashville, TN: Thomas
Nelson.

Harold J. Gardiner, S.J. 1975. "Moral Principles Towards a Definition
of the Obscene." In *The Pornography Controversy,* edited by
Ray C. Rist, 159-174. New Brunswick, NJ: Transaction.

Roberto Santiago. 1990. "Sex, Lust and Video Tapes: How
    pornography affects Black couples." *Essence* November:62+.

Pontifical Council for Social Communications. 1989.
    "Pornography and Vice in the Media." *The Pope Speaks: The
    Church Documents Bimonthly* September/October:273-278.

Jean Davidson. 1988. "What's so obscene about pornography?"
    US Catholic June:20-26.

Religious Leaders' Statements on Pornography 1986-1987.
    Morality in Media, 475 Riverside Drive, New York, NY 10115.

Pornography: Far from the Song of Songs. 1988. Louisville, KY:
    Presbyterian Church (U.S.A.).

Mary Pellauer. 1987. "Pornography: An Agenda for the Churches."
    Christian Century July 29—August 5:651-655.

Post-modern Perspectives on Sex and Pornography

Sylvere Lotringer. 1988. *Overexposed: Treating Sexual
    Perversion in America.* New York: Pantheon.

Jean Baudrillard. 1990. "The Ecliptic of Sex," in *Seduction*,
    5-49. Trans. Brian Singer. New York: St. Martins.

Dennis Giles. 1977. "Pornographic Space: The Other Place."
    In *The 1977 Film Studies Annual: Part 2*, 52-66.
    Pleasantville, NY: Redgrave.

Gertrud Koch. 1989. "The Body's Shadow Realm." Trans. Jan-
    Christopher Horak and Joyce Rheuban. *October* 50:1-29.

Claire Pajaczkowska. 1981. "The Heterosexual Presumption: A
    Contribution to the Debate on Pornography." *Screen* 22, no.
    1:79-94.

SEXUALITY

Theoretical Perspectives

Sigmund Freud. 1962. *Three Essays on the Theory of Sexuality.* Trans. James Strachey. New York: Basic.

Donald Symons. 1979. *The Evolution of Human Sexuality.* New York: Oxford UP.

John Money. 1980. *Love & Love Sickness: The Science of Sex, Gender Difference, and Pair-Bonding.* Baltimore: Johns Hopkins UP.

John Money. 1988. *Lovemaps.* Buffalo, NY: Prometheus.

Michel Foucault. 1980. *The History of Sexuality, Volume 1: An Introduction.* Trans. Robert Hurley. New York: Vintage.

John H. Gagnon and William Simon. 1973. *Sexual Conduct: The Social Sources of Human Sexuality.* Chicago: Aldine.

William Simon and John H. Gagnon. 1986. "Sexual Scripts: Permanence and Change." *Archives of Sexual Behavior* 15, no. 2:97-120.

Ethel Spector Person. 1980. "Sexuality as the Mainstay of Identity: Psychoanalytic Perspectives." *Signs* 5, no. 4:605-630.

William Masters, Virginia E. Johnson, and Robert C. Kolodny. 1988. *Masters and Johnson on Sex and Human Loving.* Boston: Little.

Jeffrey Weeks. 1981. "Sexuality and the historian." In *Sex, Politics and Society: The regulation of sexuality since 1800*, 1-18. London: Longman.

Roger Scruton. 1986. *Sexual Desire: A Moral Philosophy of the Erotic.* New York: The Free Press.

Luce Irigaray. 1985. *This Sex Which Is Not One.* Trans. Catherine Porter. Ithaca, NY: Cornell UP.

Lawrence Stone. 1985. "Sex in the West." *The New Republic* July 8:25-37.

Thomas Laqueur. 1990. *Making Sex: Body and Gender from the Greeks to Freud.* Cambridge, MA: Harvard UP.

Darker Visions

Camille Paglia. 1990. "Sex and Violence, or Nature and Art."
In *Sexual Personae: Art and Decadence from Nefertiti to
Emily Dickinson*, 1-39. New Haven, CT: Yale UP.

Georges Bataille. 1986. *Erotism: Death and Sensuality*. Trans.
Mary Dalwood. San Francisco: City Lights.

Ernest Becker. 1969. "Everyman As Pervert: An Essay on the
Pathology of Normalcy." In *Angel In Armor: A Post-Freudian
Perspective on the Nature of Man*, 1-38. New York: George
Braziller.

Alphonso Lingis. 1983. *Excesses: Eros and Culture*. Albany, NY:
State University of New York Press.

Jane E. Brody. 1990. "Scientists Trace Aberrant Sexuality."
New York Times January 23:C1+.

Masturbation:
Historical, Theological, and Philosophical Views

Vern L. Bullough and Bonnie Bullough. 1977. "The Secret Sin,"
in *Sin, Sickness, & Sanity: A History of Sexual Attitudes*,
55-73. New York: Garland.

James Hillman. 1968. "Towards the Archetypal Model for the
Masturbation Inhibition." In *The Reality of the Psyche*, edited by
Joseph B. Wheelwright, 114-127. New York: Putnam.

Thomas S. Szasz. 1970. "The New Product: Masturbatory
Insanity." In *The Manufacture of Madness*, 180-206.
New York: Harper & Row.

Andre Guindon. 1977. "Masturbation." In *The Sexual Language:
An Essay in Moral Theology*, 251-297. Ottawa: University of
Ottawa Press.

Charles E. Curran. 1970. "Masturbation and Objectively Grave
Matter." In *A New Look at Christian Morality*, 200-221.
Notre Dame, IN: Fides.

Patrick Kaler. 1982. "The Catholic View of Masturbation."
Liguorian (August):42-47.

A. W. Richard Sipe. 1990. "The Masturbations." In *A Secret
World: Sexuality and the Search for Celibacy*, 139-158.
New York: Brunner/Mazel.

Jacqueline Fortunata. 1980. "Masturbation and Women's Sexuality."
In *The Philosophy of Sex: Contemporary Readings*, edited by
Alan Soble, 389-408. Totowa, NJ: Rowman & Littlefield.

Alan Soble. 1991. "Masturbation and Sexual Philosophy." In
The Philosophy of Sex, 2nd ed., edited by Alan Soble, 133-157.
Savage, MD: Rowman & Littlefield.

Men on Sex

James B. Nelson. 1988. *The Intimate Connection: Male
Sexuality, Masculine Spirituality*. Philadelphia: Westminster.

Michael S. Kimmel, editor. 1990. *Men Confront Pornography*.
New York: Crown.

John Stoltenberg. 1989. *Refusing To Be A Man: Essays on
Sex and Justice*. New York: Meridian.

John Stoltenberg. 1984. "Refusing to be a man." *Women's
Studies Int. Forum* 7, no.1:25-27.

Jack Litewka. 1974. "The Socialized Penis." *Liberation*
March-April:16-25.

Shere Hite. 1981. *The Hite Report on Male Sexuality*. New
York: Alfred A. Knopf.

Bernie Zilbergeld. 1992. *The New Male Sexuality*. New York:
Bantam.

Sexual Science Under Review

Janice M. Irvine. 1990. *Disorders of Desire: Sex and Gender in
Modern American Sexology*. Philadelphia: Temple UP.

Janice M. Irvine. 1990. "From Difference to Sameness: Gender
    Ideology in Sexual Science." *The Journal of Sex Research*
    27, no.1:7-24.

Lisa Duggan. 1990. "From Instincts to Politics: Writing the
    History of Sexuality in the U.S." *The Journal of Sex
    Research* 27, no. 1:95-109.

Paul Robinson. 1976, 1989. *The Modernization of Sex*. Ithaca,
    NY: Cornell UP.

Andre Bejin. 1985. "The decline of the psycho-analyst and the rise of
    the sexologist." In *Western Sexuality: Practice and Precept in Past
    and Present Times*, edited by Philippe Aries and Andre Bejin,
    181-200. Trans. Anthony Forster. New York: Blackwell.

Carol A. Pollis. 1988. "An Assessment of the Impacts of
    Feminism on Sexual Science." *The Journal of Sex Research*
    25, no. 1:85-105.

Bernie Zilbergeld and Michael Evans. 1980. "The Inadequacy of
    Masters and Johnson." *Psychology Today* August:29-43.

CHRISTIANITY

Sexual Practice in Historical Perspective

Vern L. Bullough. 1976. *Sexual Variance in Society and History*.
    New York: John Wiley & Sons.

Peter Brown. 1988. *The Body and Society: Men, Women, and
    Sexual Renunciation in Early Christianity*. New York:
    Columbia UP.

James A. Brundage. 1987. *Law, Sex, and Christian Society in
    Medieval Europe*. Chicago: University of Chicago Press.

John Boswell. 1980. *Christianity, Social Tolerance, and
    Homosexuality*. Chicago: University of Chicago Press.

John T. Noonan, Jr. 1966, 1986. *Contraception: A History of Its
    Treatment by the Catholic Theologians and Canonists*.
    Cambridge, MA: Harvard UP.

Thomas N. Tentler. 1977. "Sex and the Married Penitent," in
Sin and Confession on the Eve of the Reformation, 162-232.
Princeton, NJ: Princeton UP.

Elaine Pagels. 1988. *Adam, Eve, and the Serpent.* New York: Vintage.

William Graham Cole. 1955. "Interpretations of Sex in Christianity."
In *Sex in Christianity and Psychoanalysis*, 3-195.
New York: Oxford UP.

Uta Ranke-Heinemann. 1990. *Eunuchs for the Kingdom of Heaven:
Women, Sexuality, and the Catholic Church.* Trans. Peter
Heinegg. New York: Doubleday.

Sexual Ethics

Margaret A. Farley. 1978. "Sexual Ethics." In *Encyclopedia of
Bioethics, Volume 4*, edited by Warren T. Reich, 1575-1589.
New York: Free Press.

James M. Gustafson. 1981. "Nature, Sin, and Covenant: Three
Bases for Sexual Ethics." *Perspectives in Biology and
Medicine* Spring:483-497.

Paul D. Simmons. 1987. "Theological Approaches to Sexuality: An
Overview." In *Sexuality and Medicine, Volume 2: Ethical
Viewpoints in Transition*, edited by Earl E. Shelp, 199-217.
Boston: Reidel.

Ronald M. Green. 1987. "The Irrelevance of Theology for Sexual
Ethics." In *Sexuality and Medicine, Volume 2: Ethical Viewpoints
in Transition*, edited by Earl E. Shelp, 249-270. Boston: Reidel.

Daniel C. Maguire. 1987. "Catholic Sexual and Reproductive Ethics:
A Historical Perspective." *Siecus* Report May-June:1-4.

Lisa Sowle Cahill. 1978. "Sexual Issues in Christian Theological
Ethics: A Review of Recent Studies." *Religious Studies Review*
4, no. 1:1-14.

Anthony Kosnik, et al. 1977. *Human Sexuality: New Directions
in American Catholic Thought.* New York: Paulist.

Norman J. Muckerman. 1977. "The Human Sexuality Report: Four
   Redemptorist Theologians React." *Liguorian* October:2-8.

John Paul II. 1980. "Lust and Personal Dignity." *Origins* 10:303-304.

James B. Nelson. 1983. "Sexuality Issues in American Religious
   Groups: An Update." In *Human Sexuality and the Family*,
   edited by James W. Maddock, Gerhard Neubeck, and Marvin B.
   Sussman, 35-46. New York: Haworth.

Miscellaneous Articles

Barbara Ehrenreich, Elizabeth Hess, and Gloria Jacobs. 1986.
   "Unbuckling The Bible Belt: The Christian Right Discovers
   Sex." *Mother Jones* July/August:46+.

Carol LeMasters. 1991. "Porn, pleasure, and sex." A review of
   Hard Core, by Linda Williams. *Christianity and Crisis*
   January 7:423-425.

Bob Guccione. 1987. "Art and Pornography." In *Once a Catholic*,
   edited by Peter Occhiograsso, 137-147. Boston: Houghton.

Art Harris and Jason Berry. 1988. "Jimmy Swaggart's Secret Sex
   Life." *Penthouse* July:104+.

Index

About the Author

Art Mielke was born in 1949 in Syracuse, New York. In 1971 he received his A.B. in philosophy from Bucknell University, having spent one year at the University of Glasgow in Glasgow, Scotland. In 1974 he received his M.Div. from Yale Divinity School. Following stints as a ministerial intern, Oxford University graduate student, merchant seaman, and prep school teacher, he fulfilled a long-standing desire to drive 18-wheelers. For eight years he delivered gasoline and diesel fuel on the West Coast, during which time he completed an M.A. in counseling psychology at Lewis & Clark College in Portland, Oregon. In 1987 he began work on a Ph.D. in religion at Syracuse University, completing that degree in 1991. He is currently assistant professor of philosophy and sociology at Lees College in Jackson, Kentucky.